N·E·T·S·C·A·P·E™
QUICK TOUR
FOR MACINTOSH

ACCESSING & NAVIGATING THE INTERNET'S WORLD WIDE WEB

N·E·T·S·C·A·P·E™
QUICK TOUR
FOR MACINTOSH

ACCESSING & NAVIGATING THE INTERNET'S WORLD WIDE WEB

STUART HARRIS & GAYLE KIDDER

Macintosh Graphics by Phil Hom

VENTANA
PRESS

Netscape™ Quick Tour for Macintosh: Accessing & Navigating the Internet's World Wide Web, Special Edition
Copyright © 1995 by Stuart Harris & Gayle Kidder

Library of Congress Cataloging-in-Publication Data

Harris, Stuart (Stuart H.)
    Netscape quick tour for Macintosh : accessing & navigating the Internet's world wide web / Stuart Harris & Gayle Kidder.
        p.   cm.
    Includes index.
    ISBN 1-56604-267-4
    1. Netscape (Computer file) 2. World Wide Web (Information retrieval system) 3. Internet (Computer network) I. Kidder, Gayle. II. Title.
TK5105.882.H37 1995b
025.04—dc20   94-47125
                          CIP

Book design: Marcia Webb
Cover design: Dawne Sherman, Mike Webster
Cover illustration: Dawne Sherman
Vice President, Ventana Press: Walter R. Bruce, III
Art Director: Marcia Webb
Design staff: Dawne Sherman
Editorial Manager: Pam Richardson
Editorial staff: Angela Anderson, Jonathan Cato, Tracye Giles, Beth Snowberger
Developmental Editor: Tim C. Mattson
Project Editor: Marion Laird
Print Department: Dan Koeller, Wendy Bernhardt
Product Manager: Clif McCormick
Production Manager: John Cotterman
Production staff: Lance Kozlowski, Jaimie Livingston
Index service: Dianne Bertsch, Answers Plus
Technical review: Matthew Saderholm

First Edition 9 8 7 6 5 4 3 2 1
Printed in the United States of America

Ventana Press, Inc.
P.O. Box 2468
Chapel Hill, NC 27515
919/942-0220
FAX 919/942-1140

Limits of Liability and Disclaimer of Warranty
The authors and publisher of this book have used their best efforts in preparing the book and the programs contained in it. These efforts include the development, research and testing of the theories and programs to determine their effectiveness. The authors and publisher make no warranty of any kind, expressed or implied, with regard to these programs or the documentation contained in this book.

The authors and publisher shall not be liable in the event of incidental or consequential damages in connection with, or arising out of, the furnishing, performance or use of the programs, associated instructions and/or claims of productivity gains.

TRADEMARKS

ABOUT THE AUTHORS

Stuart Harris is the author of *The irc Survival Guide* (Addison-Wesley) and numerous articles about the Internet in national magazines. He works as an Internet consultant and is leader of his local computer society's Internet special-interest group. He has also been involved in technical editing and TV documentary production and enjoys communicating complex ideas to a mass audience.

Gayle Kidder is a journalist and editor with twenty years experience in books, magazines, newspapers and documentary television. She has published over 500 articles in magazines and newspapers on topics as diverse as science, theatre, art, travel, fiction and computers. She currently maintains an online column of cultural events for the city of San Diego at **http://www.thegroup.net/kidder/otsd.htm.**

Their joint projects have included TV documentary production, journalism, software product management and, more recently, live theater on the Internet. They work in the classic "electronic cottage" in a beach area of San Diego and are on the Net every day of their lives.

ACKNOWLEDGMENTS

We consider ourselves lucky to have had a number of bright and capable Net wizards who cheerfully helped us in our writing of this book. Foremost among them is our colleague Phil Hom of Primus Inc. Phil turned out to know a few tricks with his Mac that we didn't know, resulting in the superior quality of illustration in this book.

We also thank sysadmin Mark Burgess of the Data Transfer Group in San Diego, a prince among Webmasters, for his unfailing generosity and expert guidance (and for giving us our first copy of Netscape).

Mike Bowen at CERFnet provided invaluable assistance on several topics. Brent Halliburton of Group Cortex, and Steve Sanders of the CyberSpace DataBase BBS, contributed undocumented features.

Thanks also go to Gareth Branwyn for giving us, in his forerunning books about Mosaic, a good model to follow.

Last but not least, we'd like to acknowledge each other. Neither of us thinks there's the slightest chance we could have turned this book out on schedule without the other's help and support.

CONTENTS

INTRODUCTION xvii

THE NET & THE WEB 1

The Internet: Who's in Charge? 2

The World Wide Web 4

What's a Web Page? 6

Netscape Navigator: Your Window on the Web 7

GETTING STARTED 11

Necessary Connections 12
   Your TCP/IP Stack • Other Programs You May Need

Downloading Netscape 14
   Using Fetch to Download Netscape Navigator • Using
   Traditional FTP on a Dial-Up Account

Unpacking & Installing Your Programs 18
    Installing StuffIt Expander • Unpacking Netscape
    • Installing Netscape
Getting Set Up 20
    Setting Basic Preferences
Netscape Quick Peek 22
    Using URLs • Plugging Into Your Own Home Page

 MENUS, BUTTONS & BARS **27**

The Toolbar: Navigating in Netscape 28
    Back • Forward • Home • Reload • Images • Open • Print
    • Find • Stop
Main Menu Bar 32
    File • Edit • View • Go • Options • Directory • Help
Directory Buttons 45
Mouse tricks 46
Activity & Location Indicators 47
    The URL Window • Title bar • Progress Bar • Security Key
    • Status Indicator (Logo)
How to Use Bookmarks 50
    Creating Your First Few Bookmarks • Categorizing Bookmark
    Lists • Adding Headers & Separators • Other Bookmark
    Options • Turning Your Bookmark List Into a Web Page
    • Exporting & Importing Bookmarks

Setting Special Preferences 56
Window & Link Styles • Fonts & Colors • Mail & News • Cache
& Network • Applications & Directories • Images & Security
• Proxies • Helper Applications • Customizing Netscape for
Multiple Users

4 LAUNCHING INTO CYBERSPACE 63

Hypermedia in Netscape 64
Still Photos: .GIFs & .JPEGs • Still Photos: In-Lines & Externals
• QuickTime & MPEG Movies • Audio • Forms

Exploring Cyberspace 69
Electronic Publications • News & Sports • Museums & Art
Galleries • Educational Resources • Government & Institutions
• Business & Commercial • Databases • Movies &
Entertainment • Travel • Personal Home Pages

Internet Services via Netscape..79
E-Mail • FTP • Gopher • TELNET • USENET Newsgroups
• Archie • Finger

Staying Current 88
Getting Updates • FAQs & Other Reading Material
• Information Sites • Newsgroups

5 MAKING YOUR OWN WEB DOCUMENTS 91

HTML: The Language of the Web 91
Building a Home Page 93

Adding Images & Links 97
    Links • How We Raided the Louvre... And They'll
    Never Catch Us!

Testing Your Page 104

Posting Your Page 105

Web Page Design Tips 106

SPECIAL APPLICATIONS & SITES 109

Web-Searching Tips 110

Our Favorite Web Searchers 112
    The WebCrawler • Harvest • Lycos • World Wide Web Worm
    (WWWW) • The CUI W3 Catalog • The Great Burgundy Quest

Prize-Winning Web Pages 117
    The Best of the Web • Global Network Navigator • ArtServe
    • London's Natural History Museum • The Virtual Hospital
    • Travels With Samantha • The Constitution of the United States
    of America • Expo • Restaurant Le Cordon Bleu • The Virtual
    Tourist • Welcome to the Globewide Network Academy
    • Arctic Adventours, Inc. • The Branch Mall • The Hypertext
    Webster • Current Weather Maps/Movies • The Electronic
    Frontier Foundation • Paris • Sliding Tiles Puzzles • The Virtual
    Radio • Fairy Tales • alt.binaries made EZ • Icon Browsers
    • The Global Village Idiot • URouLette

APPENDIX A **UNDOCUMENTED FEATURES OF NETSCAPE NAVIGATOR** 125

Different Strokes for Different Folks • What Does the N Do? • Who Was That Masked Programmer? • Netscape's House Organ • Secure Pages to Order • GIF Retrieval • Hypertext Newsgroup Reading

APPENDIX B **COMMON NETSCAPE ERROR MESSAGES** 129

Unable to locate the server • Not found • 404 Not found • 403 Forbidden • Connection refused by host • Helper application not found • File contains no data • Too many users • Bad File Request • TCP error encountered while sending request to server. • Failed DNS lookup • NNTP Server error • Cannot add form submission result to bookmark list

APPENDIX C **ABOUT THE ONLINE COMPANION** 133

GLOSSARY 135

INDEX 147

INTRODUCTION

The recent explosion of interest in the Internet for personal use amounts to a headlong rush toward a new global culture. As more and more people discover the ease and speed of e-mail and the vast wellspring of information to be tapped at the touch of a key or the click of a mouse, it is as if a virtual city were being built out of thin air—overnight.

Nothing has made the resources of the Internet more accessible to ordinary people all over the world than that part of the Internet known as the World Wide Web. Born only six years ago, in 1989, as the by-product of a European physics lab in Switzerland, the World Wide Web now links together hundreds of thousands of documents all over the world, including not just scientific but educational, business, commercial and recreational interests as well.

The latest, hippest window on the ever-changing scenery of the Web is Netscape Navigator, a software package that allows you not only to browse the Web with ease but to take advantage of all the other Internet resources with one easy interface. Netscape Navigator is the first commercial offshoot of Mosaic, the U.S. Government-developed product. Netscape used the talents of many of the bright young programmers who developed Mosaic, and it offers the same easy visual format, allowing the user to quickly search through documents and skip lightly from one to another in pursuit of items of personal interest.

The first time you set off to explore the World Wide Web is something like entering a magic hall of mirrors. Every time you turn a corner or open a new door, another world opens up for you. One moment you may be in Boston, the next you're in Santa Cruz. Then at the touch of a mouse you're off to Tokyo, Stockholm, London, Hong Kong.

This is the amazing metauniverse that the World Wide Web has created in just a few short years. And every day, as more and more people discover the Web and begin to imagine its possibilities, it becomes even richer. In fact, the Internet has been so democratized by the advent of the Web that a student in Arkansas can now create his or her own "page" on the Web that has standing equal to that of the Smithsonian Institution or the White House visitors' page.

In writing this guide to Netscape Navigator, which cannot help but be a guide to the Web as well, we are thinking of our typical reader as reasonably well educated but not necessarily technically inclined. Our target reader may be a teacher or a business person who wants to tap into the resources on the Web but has little time to spend learning a complex software program—the sort of person Netscape Navigator was designed for, actually. He or she may well need help getting Netscape Navigator set up—a task comparable in difficulty to programming a modern VCR (which often sends parents to their kids for help). But our prototype reader is above all someone who is ready to explore the Web with us and have some fun while picking up valuable information.

We assume that you already have at least an elementary understanding of the Internet, although that may not extend much beyond e-mail. Readers who feel a need for more background on the Internet are advised to pick up one of the many great books on the market now, such as Michael Fraase's *Mac Internet Tour Guide* (Ventana Press), or *The Whole Internet Book* or *Big Dummy's Guide to the Internet*. Once you've got Netscape Navigator installed, you'll be able to find excerpts from the latter two of these titles on the Web.

Hardware & Software Requirements

Before we start, there are some basic hardware and software requirements to be met. "Uh oh," we hear you saying, "here it comes—another upgrade." Not necessarily. Naturally, as with most powerful programs these days, the bigger your hard drive and the more RAM you have, the smoother things will be for you.

But if you've got the basics, there's no reason to run out and buy more until you explore the Web and see what kind of information you'll want to access. It's perfectly possible to run Netscape Navigator with a minimal configuration as long as you're not in a hurry or you're willing to do without the images much of the time. Here's what we recommend:

- Mac System 7 or better with at least 4mb RAM (8mb is better).
- A 68020 processor or better (Netscape will not run on the Mac Plus, SE, Classic, Portable, or PowerBook 100).
- 14,400 baud modem or faster (will work with 9600 but will probably be intolerably slow).
- A color monitor, the higher the definition the better (not necessary to access the Web but recommended if you want to take full advantage of image capability).
- A TCP/IP stack (MacTCP) and TCP connection software (MacSLIP, MacPPP or InterSLIP).

In addition, you should make sure you have about 20mb of free hard-drive space. Netscape will need it for creating temporary directories.

And last, but most important, you will need your Internet connection—either a direct connection through your institution or business or a SLIP/PPP connection that can be arranged through a private access provider. We'll go into this in more detail in Chapter 2.

Super-Duper Quick Start

Netscape Navigator is easy to set up and begin to use on your own, providing you have a working familiarity with communications software. If your Internet connection is already up and running, simply remove the disk from the back of this book and follow the instructions to install Netscape. In the process of installation it should take account of any helper applications you already have that Netscape can use.

Then click on the Netscape logo and you're off! Netscape will take you to its own Welcome page, and from there you can follow links to whatever interests you. For some interesting sites to visit, check out What's New? and What's Cool? on the Directory buttons (or in the Directory pull-down on the main menu).

Take a look around and enjoy yourself. After a while we're sure you'll want to know more about some of Netscape's special features. Jump ahead to Chapters 3 through 6 to learn how to get helper applications, use the Bookmarks menu, do searches and use Netscape for FTP, TELNET and USENET newsreading. And since you're a quick learner, we know you'll want to take a look at the "undocumented features" in the back of the book—things you can do that the handbook doesn't tell you.

What's Inside

Chapter 1, "The Net & the Web," provides a brief look at the development of the Web as the newest and fastest-growing segment of the Internet. It explains how the idea of hypermedia in an easy-to-use graphical interface transformed a system once used primarily by the techno-elite into a new democratic forum.

Chapter 2, "Getting Netscape," tells you how to get updated versions of Netscape along with any subsidiary programs you may need, and it gives explicit instructions on downloading via FTP. You'll learn how to install Netscape and how to set it up once you have it. Then we'll take a quick Web cruise through Netscape's main features.

Chapter 3, "Menus, Buttons & Bars," gives a detailed tour of Netscape Navigator's menu items and its easy-to-use buttons. We'll tell you how you can use Netscape's Bookmarks menu to keep track of your favorite Web pages. And we'll guide you in configuring Netscape for reading USENET newsgroups, sending e-mail and doing other things you're interested in on the Internet.

Chapter 4, "Launching Into Cyberspace," begins by looking closely at hypermedia on the Web, explaining what you need to play audio files and view movies with Netscape Navigator. Then we'll look at the different kinds of Web documents available for all interests, including online publications, educational resources, museums and art galleries, business sites, travel and recreation and much more. Finally we'll explain how to use Netscape to do other special applications like FTP, TELNET and reading the USENET news.

Chapter 5, "Making Your Own Web Documents," is a brief primer on designing a Web page. We'll show you visually how we created a simple home page, with easy steps you can follow in designing your own Web document.

Chapter 6, "Special Applications & Sites," explains how to use the Web to search for topics that interest you. Then we'll point you to some prize-winning Web sites and some of our personal favorites to get you started on your own explorations.

Also, we've included two appendices: one on undocumented Netscape features and the other on common error messages. And you'll find a comprehensive glossary and index for your reference.

As a special addition, you can go to the Netscape Online Companion, where you can find the software you need to enhance your enjoyment of hypermedia on the Web, and hypertext links to all the hot sites mentioned in this book.

Nothing Stays the Same

When we got our first copy of Netscape Navigator—a Version 0.9 beta release—we were immediately impressed with its superior features, its speed and its friendly interface to dozens of applications. During the first writing of this book, Netscape went through three subsequent beta versions to the official Version 1.0 release. Only a few months later we found ourselves revising it yet again for the Version 1.1, upon which this edition is based. We've seen a couple of minor screen changes, some diligent bug-chasing, and impressive improvements in the Newsgroup reader and the highly efficient caching system—all that stuff that is supposed to go on behind the scenes without your having to worry about it.

Most likely there are more changes to come. But we feel confident that you will continue to find this a helpful guide to all the main features of Netscape Navigator, and that all the things you learn here will be easily translatable to later versions of the software.

The future of the Web is another matter. It is changing so rapidly day by day that it's hard to say where it will all lead six months, a year, two years from now. What is certain is that once you start looking at the Web with Netscape, you'll be as much a part of its future as physicists in Geneva, businessmen in Tokyo and high-school students in Tuscaloosa.

Stuart Harris
Gayle Kidder
San Diego, California

THE NET & THE WEB

The world of personal computing these days is a lot like the Red Queen's kingdom in "Through the Looking Glass"—everyone seems to be running faster and faster to stay in the same place. Relatively new computer users can be forgiven for fearing that they'll never catch up.

If you've gotten as far as acquiring Netscape Navigator and buying this book, however, cheer up. You can congratulate yourself for being on the leading edge of the fastest-growing segment of the Internet—the World Wide Web.

As you begin to explore the Web with Netscape Navigator, the number of resources you'll find there may make you think this has been going on for a long time. How could you have missed out for so long? Relax—it's not so. Almost everything you see now on the Web didn't exist in 1990.

The Web itself wasn't created until 1989. But it did not become widely accessible to those outside the scientific and academic communities until the creation of the Mosaic graphical interface in 1993. It was that event which suddenly made the Web easily available and attractive to hundreds of thousands of computer users around the world. This set of statistics gives you the idea: in June 1993, there were 130 server sites on the Web; by November 1994, approximately a year and a half later, there were more than 10,000. Multiply by the number of people logging in at all those sites and you can see where we're going.

Given the rapidly growing interest in the World Wide Web for educational and commercial uses, it's entirely possible that this is your first experience with "that thing" everyone's been talking about for the last few years, the Internet. And you may be wondering, "How does the Internet relate to the Web?" If you're confused about the difference, read on (don't be embarrassed, nobody's looking over your shoulder now, right?).

By the end of this chapter, you should have a fairly clear idea of the world you're entering with Netscape Navigator. By the end of this book, we hope you'll be running alongside the rest of us in the world of computing, trying to keep up with the changes that are hitting us faster every day.

The Internet: Who's in Charge?

Basically, the Internet is the architecture upon which everything else you've heard about hangs. It is nothing more (and nothing less) than thousands of computers all over the world that communicate with each other minute-by-minute over an unbelievably complicated network of cables, fiberoptic filaments and satellite links.

Although it started—back in the Info Stone Age of the '60s—as a creation of the U.S. Government, it's important to realize that the Internet as it exists today belongs to no one country, government or business, no matter how large or powerful, nor is it operated by any single authority.

"So who's in charge?" you might rightly ask. Well, nobody and everybody.

It works something like this: Imagine that you live at the northwest corner of an unbelievably complex network of canals. You need to send a message to somebody at the southeast corner. There may be 1,000 different routes your message could take on its way from one corner to the other, and you have no way of knowing which might be the best—which canals are congested right now, which have been taken out of service for maintenance, which have been blocked by a bus or a large animal falling in. Nevertheless, you can put your message in a bottle, label the bottle "SE" and just toss it into the nearest canal. You can walk away confident that your message will get through as long as there's an agreement between the people who live on this canal system.

The agreement is this: At every canal junction there's a person who knows which routes are blocked in the immediate neighborhood. This person picks up each bottle that comes by, looks at its label, and sends it off down a canal that's relatively free-flowing and going in the right direction. Oh, and one more thing—the bottles are rather small, so if you have a big message you must break it into parts labeled A,B,C... da-da-dah, and put each part in a separate bottle. And there's no guarantee that all of those parts will take the same route or even arrive in sequential order.

You can readily imagine that as long as everyone plays by the rules, your message will get through and be put back together into one piece, even if there is *nobody at all who understands the complete network*. That key idea, that a network could function without any minute-by-minute overall control by a mastermind, was absolutely revolutionary when it was first suggested. The idea has proven to be much more than just a very good solution to a tough technical problem: it has become a way of thinking that explains a lot about the Internet "culture."

So, when you use Netscape to go and find a document in Stockholm or a picture in Mexico City, and it takes half a minute or so for it all to arrive, you can imagine it as thousands of little bottles, sedately floating your way down a maze of "cybercanals."

The World Wide Web

User-friendliness wasn't an issue back in the '60s when the military and the scientists wove together the first strands of what would become the Internet. If you couldn't enter something like *deroff -w detail.list | tr A-Z a-z | sort | uniq >detail.sorted* at a UNIX prompt, you didn't belong. The people who created, maintained and used the Net were so comfortable with that kind of language, they would use it to talk to each other over the breakfast table. (*"Deroff -w the coffee machine while you're up, would you, dear?"*)

There was absolutely no need for user-friendliness until large numbers of users outside the university system came along. That's why all the great strides down the road to the "ultimate killer app" have been taken in this decade, the '90s.

The World Wide Web is certainly one of those strides. Once it became possible to instantly access hundreds of thousands of documents all over the world, it was only logical to think it possible to skip lightly from one related document to the next without laborious search-and-find operations. The World Wide Web made that possible by means of "hypertext."

Hypertext was an idea waiting to happen ever since the first writer created the first footnote. This is how it works:

Say you're helping your child devise a science project. She's interested in spiders, so that's a start. You go together to the library and find a book on spiders. She finds an interesting section about spiders who eat their own mates or young. That sparks an interest in cannibalism among insects in general. You notice a footnote reference to a book about cannibalism in insects. So you pull down that book, find the appropriate section, and as you're reading you become interested in the curious habits of praying mantises. Here's something you might find in your own back yard and use for an experiment. So you follow yet another bibliographic reference to a book on praying mantises.

If you were using the World Wide Web, all of this running back and forth to library shelves, jumping from book to book, would be made very easy for you. In the initial document on spiders you might see a "hypertext link" to cannibalism in insects—i.e., "cannibalism in insects" would appear highlighted in color in the text. By clicking on the highlighted link, you would go directly to the referenced document. From there, you might follow another hypertext link to "praying mantises." Whenever you find anything you want to keep, you can save it to a file on your own computer. It isn't even necessary to know the location of documents you obtain this way—the address is embedded in the text. Obviously, though, you have to have a starting point.

Now let's say you could click on a picture of a female praying mantis and watch it devour its mate in a short video. You might also press an audio button to hear her crunch, crunch, crunch (if you really wanted to). Now you've gone beyond hypertext to *hypermedia*.

Once it became possible to transmit not only text but pictures and audio and movie files, and PC technology reached the stage where they could easily be displayed, the Web—as you can see in Figure 1-1— became truly hypermedia.

So we reach the point where we are today, when computer industry titans slug it out with Hollywood moguls on the business pages of newspapers every morning to see who will be the first to deliver to you full-scale home videos, among other things, by a click of the mouse.

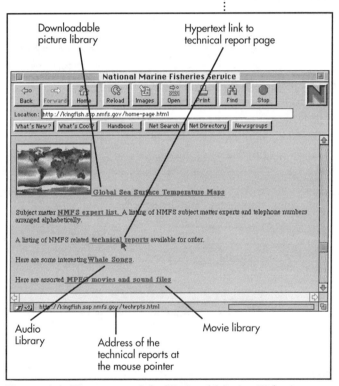

Figure 1-1: *Home page of the National Marine Fisheries Service: a good example of a hypermedia page.*

What's a Web Page?

You'll hear lots of references to "Web pages" in Net talk. The term can be confusing to a newcomer. A Web page is merely a document designed to be accessed and read over the World Wide Web. It must have an address in a recognized format—the URL, or Uniform Resource Locator—that enables computers all over the world to locate it. Each Web page has its own unique URL. The term "page" arises naturally because of the visual similarity of a Web document onscreen to a printed page. However, there are important differences to bear in mind, apart from the obvious one: these so-called "pages" have no fixed width, height, weight or physical location. A Web page is actually a data document that has been encoded in ways very similar to typesetting, using a simple code language called HTML (stands for HyperText Markup Language). The code says things like "put a picture here," "make this a header" and "start a paragraph here." It also includes codes that say "put a link here to another document."

All of this code is meant to be interpreted and presented to your screen by a "Web browser." It's your Web browser, as much as the code embedded in the page itself, that actually tells your computer how to display the encoded information—the font to display text in, the screen layout to use—and that in turn is to a certain extent under your personal control. Netscape Navigator is merely one of several Web browsers currently available, albeit one of the newest and most versatile.

Who or What Is Mozilla? Users of Mosaic and lurkers around the USENET groups devoted to the latest developments may have picked up some of the early rumors about a new Web browser called Mozilla. Mozilla was simply the name the young programmers at the University of Illinois at Urbana-Champaign who designed Mosaic gave to their next-generation browser while they were developing it.

The pet name in the programming department was squelched by the marketing department at Netscape Communications Corporation—which was also persuaded by strong-armed attorneys representing the NCSA and the State of Illinois to give up its own first-choice name as Mosaic Communications Corporation.

The more "traditional" stuff of the Internet—FTP and WAIS and USENET and TELNET and the Gopher—has not gone away. It keeps on growing, and actually much of it can be read by Web software. In the early days of the Web, it could be said (and it was) that the Web was not so much a new part of the Internet as a new way of *looking at* what was there all the time. With the proliferation of "pages" specifically designed for Web browsing, that no longer holds true. But, certainly, nobody thinks we are anywhere close to being able to do away with the information that is cataloged in the more traditional ways. On the contrary, there's a clear trend for the graphical Web browsers to include more and more of those other Internet access tools wrapped in ever fancier and friendlier packages. Netscape is squarely in the mainstream of that trend.

Netscape Navigator: Your Window on the Web

When Samuel Morse invented the telegraph, making it possible for stations throughout a railroad's network to get instant information about the running of the trains, people didn't say "Yeah, sure—this may look good right now. But just wait until the telephone comes out. It'll make this collection of wires and keys look like junk overnight." No, obviously the natural reaction to any advance is to rejoice in its benefits and to think that, in the words of the popular song from *Oklahoma!*, "...they've gone about as fer as they can go."

The Deluxe Internet Package Netscape Navigator is a full-featured Web browser, which means that it is designed to operate as your principal, if not only, interface with the Internet. If you are already an experienced Internet cruiser, you may have favorite software programs for certain operations, such as reading USENET news or sending and receiving e-mail. You may, of course, elect to continue using these programs. But it will be possible to do most of these operations within Netscape itself.

With Netscape Navigator you can do all these things:

- access and view Web pages posted anywhere in the world.
- view images (in .GIF, .JPEG and .XBM formats) using Netscape's built-in viewer or a helper application like JPEGView.
- play audio and video files using helper applications like Sound Machine and Sparkle.
- download and save text, picture, audio and video files to your own computer.
- read and post to USENET news groups. →

So it was with NCSA Mosaic, which was such an utterly different view of the Internet that it really seemed to be the be-all and end-all. Wow!! In-line pictures!! Wow!! Instant movies!! Wow!!! Clickable hypertext links!!! WOW!!!!! WOW!!!!! WOW!!!!! It would have sold like hot cakes had it not been the product of a United States Government lab, the National Center for Supercomputing Applications (NCSA) in Illinois. As it is, Uncle Sam does not deal in hot cakes, and the software is free to anyone who can figure out how to download it.

- send e-mail anywhere (but not receive—for that you'll need an accompanying mail program).
- search the Internet using Gopher, WAIS, Archie, Veronica and a whole host of "web crawlers."
- download files using FTP.

But certain entrepreneurs, who do deal in hot cakes, looked at the "gold rush" of people downloading Mosaic and thought "Hmmmm... maybe if we improved on this and put it on the market...."

The Netscape Corporation started by hiring away most of the young computer whizzes who as undergraduates at Urbana-Champaign had

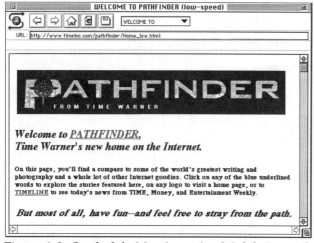

Figure 1-2: *On the left, Mosaic version 2.0alpha7—on the right, Netscape version 1.0. Can you tell it's the same design team at work?*

designed Mosaic. They set them to work designing a new Web browser that would not just cruise the Web but become an all-inclusive Internet package. Figure 1-2 shows how the design evolved from Mosaic to Netscape. How successful they've been you'll be able to judge for yourself once you get going. At this stage in its development the company welcomes feedback, and by the responses we've gotten to our queries so far, we can report they do pay attention. In the next chapter we'll tell you how to get started with Netscape and join the next wave of the Internet evolution.

Moving On

First, a quick review of the terms we've thrown at you in this chapter. For others you're not familiar with that aren't covered here, please check the Glossary at the back of this book:

The Internet is a worldwide collection of computers that communicate with one another over cables, satellites, optical fibers and phones—literally, the whole hardware mass.

The World Wide Web, or WWW, is a system designed to access documents online over the Internet. It makes it possible to read and exchange text, images, sound and video.

Hypertext and hypermedia are what the Web uses to link documents related to each other, allowing the reader to follow connections from one document to the next. Hypermedia is a more appropriate term when links are to audio and video files.

A Web Page is a document designed to be read over the World Wide Web, written with embedded codes for display instructions.

HTML, or HyperText Markup Language, is the coding Web documents or "pages" use to tell a Web browser how to display a text file.

URL, or Uniform Resource Locator, is the address of a file posted on the Web. It tells your Web browser on what machine to find the file and provides the full file pathway.

Netscape Navigator is a "Web browser," a program that allows you to explore the Web. It is an outgrowth of the popular NCSA Mosaic program. It is designed not only to read and display Web documents but to be a full-featured interface for most operations you might want to do on the Internet.

Now put down your pencil, turn on your computer and get ready. We're about to take a trip on a silicon chip into the future of the information age.

GETTING STARTED

If you're already Net-savvy, it's a safe bet that Chapter 1 didn't delay you long—and that's fine with us. So now that we're all up to speed, we can start to get organized.

In the style of the latest, most up-to-date software, Netscape Navigator is a breeze to set up, pretty much installing itself on your system. But first you need to pay attention to a few details in getting your system ready to operate.

In this chapter we'll tell you what you need to run Netscape, how to obtain the latest copy of Netscape Navigator by FTP (including updates to the version on the disk in the back of the book), as well as other applications you might need, and how to install Netscape on your computer and set basic preferences. Then we'll fire up the engines and give you a quick look at the Web pages where you can learn more about Netscape Navigator and the Web, and, finally, launch you on your first round-the-world cruise on the World Wide Web.

Necessary Connections

To run Netscape Navigator you will need either a direct Internet connection (such as that used by universities, government offices and some businesses) or you will need to set up a SLIP (Serial Line Internet Protocol) or PPP (Point-to-Point Protocol) connection with a private provider. These are getting easier and cheaper to get every day.

Many online access providers now offer a complete kit of all the software you need, preconfigured for their system, to get set up on the Web. The kit may include Netscape Navigator and the TCP/IP stack you need to make your connection to the Internet. If you're shopping for a provider, you might ask about this and, all other things being equal, choose one who will go this extra step for you.

If you're putting it all together yourself, you will need a little patience. It sometimes takes several trial-and-error attempts at setting things up before you have your communications package running smoothly. Your sysadmin (if you have one) will be your best advisor through this process—he or she knows the system better than you'll ever need to. It is outside the scope of this book to go into the details of configuring your system for communications since there are too many variations to cover. But we'll just try to point you in the right direction for what you'll need.

> **Peter Kaminsky's List of Internet Service Providers**
> For an updated electronic list of Internet service providers, Peter Kaminski's PDIAL list is highly recommended. To get a current copy of the list, send an email message to **info-deli-server@netcom.com** with the message **Send PDIAL**. If you do not yet have Net access, and therefore cannot get this list, have a wired friend download it for you.

Your TCP/IP Stack

To make your connection to the Internet you will need a TCP/IP stack. This is a program that acts as an intermediary—dialing your access provider and managing the data exchange between your computer and the Internet.

If you have previously used Mosaic, you should already have MacTCP set up and you can skip this section. If you're setting up for the first time, you'll need to get MacTCP (included in Mac System 7.5) and also TCP-based connection software—either MacSLIP, MacPPP or Interslip. If you don't have the necessary software, probably the best way to get it is with one of the Internet book-software packages such as the *Mac Internet Tour Guide* published by Ventana, which can also help you in configuring the software.

Other Programs You May Need

Netscape's binary encoded files will have to be decoded to install on your system. For this you will need another program on your system called StuffIt Expander. If you have the FTP program Fetch, it will take care of sending it over to StuffIt for unpacking for you with its Automatic File Opening feature. If you don't already have StuffIt Expander and Fetch, you can get both of them by FTP. To install StuffIt Expander, you'll also need BinHex. Try the following sites for all of these programs, including your TCP/IP stack if you need it:

- bitsy.mit.edu/pub/mac
- mac.archive.umich.edu/mac/util/comm
- ftp.cam.org/systems/mac/mactcp
- mirror.archive.umich.edu

The last address above will automatically connect you to one of a number of other mirror sites (see the Glossary). For instructions on downloading files via FTP, see "Downloading Netscape," coming up shortly.

Mirror Sites Mirror sites are other computer centers which by agreement make the same software available publicly for downloading. Any changes made to the main site are soon "reflected" by the mirror sites. Here's a list of sites where Netscape Navigator is currently available. The first part of the address (before the first slash) is the site; everything following the first slash is the directory structure.

- ftp.netscape.com
- ftp.digital.com/pub/net/infosys/Netscape
- src.doc.ic.ac.uk/packages/Netscape
- unix.hensa.ac.uk/pub/netscape
- ftp.luth.se/pub/infosystems/www/netscape
- ftp.riken.go.jp/pub/WWW/netscape
- ftp.adelaide.edu.au/pub/WWW/Netscape

Normally you should choose a site close to you for the best access. If you don't know what the addresses mean, simply avoid suffixes like *uk* and *au* for United Kingdom and Australia, for instance. On the other hand, we've found accessing Australia or Japan when it's the middle of the night there to be a good strategy sometimes.

Note: *Not all of these mirror sites necessarily have the most up-to-date version of Netscape.*

Getting and installing Fetch on your system first will make your life a lot easier. Conveniently, many of the same sites also carry Netscape Navigator, so you may be able to get everything you need with one-stop Internet shopping. The down side is that accessing some of the most popular sites can be like shopping in the bargain basement at Macy's after Christmas—you can't get through the crowd. That's why we give you more than one site to try here and several more for Netscape in the sidebar.

Downloading Netscape

Netscape Communications Corporation keeps the most recent version of Netscape Navigator posted at its FTP site, where it is available for downloading over any Internet connection. A number of unofficial mirror sites also carry the software, but not all will have the most recent version. (See the sidebar on mirror sites.) According to the license agreement for Version 1.1, the software is free for use by educational and nonprofit institutions and for evaluation by commercial users. You can get information on registering your copy and getting support once you have Netscape installed.

You can get a copy of the software using either Fetch or conventional FTP. If you already have a SLIP/PPP account and have been using Mosaic, you can download Netscape Navigator using Mosaic's FTP feature, but this is only advisable if you have a later version of Mosaic (Mosaic's earlier versions are much slower than using conventional FTP).

Note: You can obtain Netscape Navigator using a dial-up shell account and set it up on your computer. However, in order to use Netscape with anything other than local files (files in your own computer or network), you will need a SLIP/PPP connection or a direct Internet connection.

Using Fetch to Download Netscape Navigator

If you have your SLIP/PPP connection, you can use Fetch to download Netscape and it will do all the necessary file conversion for you. We'll use Netscape Communications Corporation's FTP site for our example, but you can substitute any of the addresses listed in the mirror sites sidebar.

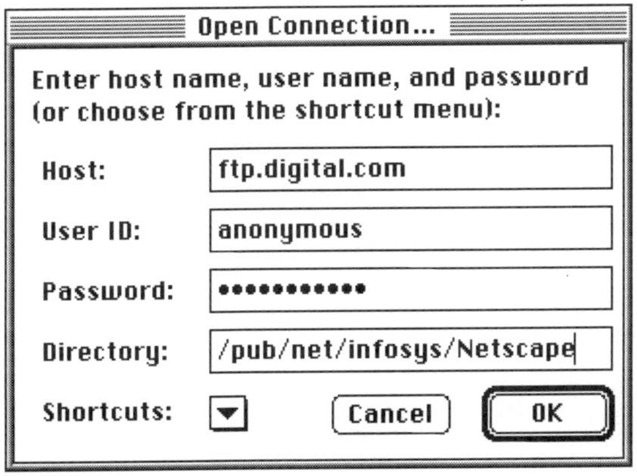

1. Log onto your account in the usual manner, then launch the program by clicking on the Fetch icon.

2. The Open Connection dialog box will appear. Make sure the Automatic file opener feature is on (indicated by the radio buttons in the lower right corner of the Fetch screen—see Figure 2-2).

3. Type **ftp.netscape.com** in the appropriate box for Host and **netscape/mac** in the Directory box. If you're using a mirror site, you'll enter the part of the address before the first slash in the Host window and the rest of the address after the slash in the Directory window. In the User ID box type **anonymous** and in the Password box, type your e-mail address. (See Figure 2-1.)

4. Choose the OK button. You'll soon be connected to the server at Netscape Communications Corporation (or your mirror site).

Figure 2-1: *The Open Connection dialog box tells Fetch where to go to find your file.*

5. Once you are connected to the remote site, the File Browser dialog box will appear. If you don't see the files you want at first, scroll through the directory structure until you do. At a very big site this can be something like winding your way down through a multistory subterranean parking structure looking for a parking spot. When you reach the right directory, you'll see a list of files available for downloading, which include

    LICENSE   **netscape-1.1.hqx**   **README**

You needn't bother downloading the license agreement or the readme file, since both will come with the main software package.

6. Choose the folder you want to download Netscape to on your computer. Highlight the Netscape file, then click on the Get File button. The file will begin to transfer to your computer. (See Figure 2-2.)

7. When it is finished transferring, you can scroll back through the directory structure for any other files you might need and repeat the procedure. When you're done, click on the Close Connection button to disconnect from the server.

Back home, Netscape Navigator will be automatically unpacked in the folder you specified.

Using Traditional FTP on a Dial-Up Account

If you have a regular dial-up shell account, you can obtain Netscape using FTP or ncftp. You can first try accessing Netscape Communications Corporation directly to download from there. But in all likelihood, due to heavy use, you'll be referred to one of the other sites where Netscape is also available. You can save time by choosing a mirror site now from the listings in the previous sidebar.

We'll use Netscape Navigator's FTP site for our example, but you can substitute any of the addresses listed.

1. Use your regular communications program to log onto your account.

2. At the prompt, type **ftp ftp.netscape.com** (or **ncftp ftp.netscape.com**). If you already have an FTP or ncftp prompt, you'll type

    open ftp.netscape.com

Note: If you're accessing a mirror site, you'll type the part of the address before the first slash. Note that for some of the sites this means you'll be typing "ftp" again as part of the address.

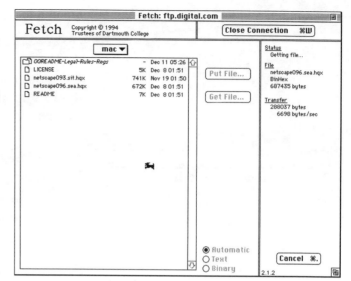

Figure 2-2: Tell Fido to "fetch" and he'll bring that file home for you.

3. Enter and you'll soon be connected to the remote server. If you're using FTP, log onto the system as "anonymous" and give your e-mail address as the password. If you're using ncftp, you won't have to (it's done for you).

4. Change the directory to the place where the current version of Netscape Navigator for Mac is available. (Everything that follows the first slash in the FTP address is the directory structure.) At Netscape Communications Corporation the full address is

ftp.netscape.com/netscape/mac

so the command would be **cd netscape/mac.**

With some of the longer addresses in the mirror sites, finding the right directory may be a bit more labyrinthine (they sometimes change). Just remember that at any point in the directory structure, you can ask for a list of files or subdirectories with the "ls" command. The command "ls -l" will give you a fuller description of contents, which sometimes helps in figuring out what you want.

5. Once you've accessed the right directory, the next screen you may see is a fairly fearsome warning against downloading Netscape for exportation to a list of countries to which the U.S. bans technology exports. By now you may be feeling like a spy, but don't worry. Everything you're doing is perfectly legal as long as you're not an enemy national.

Type **ls**, press Enter and you'll see a list of files available for downloading, which will include

LICENSE   netscape.1.1.hqx   **README**

You needn't bother downloading the license agreement or the README file, since both will come with the main software package. See Figure 2-3.

6. Now type

get netscape.1.1.hqx

or whatever the latest version is called. The file will begin to transfer to your local host computer. When it is done transferring, back up the directory tree and find whatever other programs you want and repeat the procedure. When you're done, type **quit**.

7. If you're on a dial-up account, you will have to download the file once again from the host computer to your own home computer.

> *Note: The procedure for downloading a file from the host computer to your own machine may differ according to the communications program you're using and the type of service you have. If you don't know how to do that, consult your communications program manual or ask your sysadmin.*

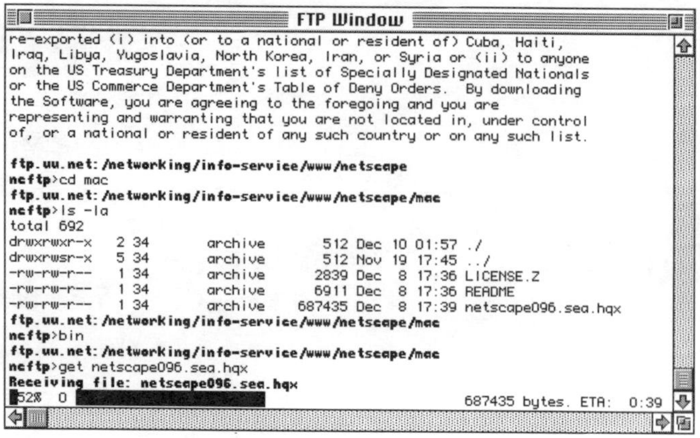

Figure 2-3: Downloading Netscape the old-fashioned way—using ncftp in a UNIX shell.

Unpacking & Installing Your Programs

If you used Fetch to get Netscape Navigator, it will have unpacked it for you already (using StuffIt Expander) into a file called Netscape Installer and you can skip off to the next section, "Installing Netscape." But if you've downloaded Netscape via conventional FTP, you will need to unpack it using StuffIt Expander. If this is part of the booty you've just obtained in your FTP raid, you'll need BinHex to install StuffIt Expander, and that should also be part of your booty.

Stufflt Expander™

Installing Stufflt Expander

After you've downloaded BinHex, you'll be ready to install StuffIt. The .hqx at the end of the file name for StuffIt indicates that the file has been compressed in binary code and stored as a text file. You'll have to tell Binhex to work its magic. Think of this step as reversing the spell to turn the frog into a prince.

1. Simply double-click on the BinHex icon to open it. Dismiss the introduction screen with another click.

2. Go to the File menu and select Download->Application. A dialog box will pop up asking you what you want to un-binhex.

3. Select the StuffIt Expander file and choose Open.

4. BinHex will ask where you want to save StuffIt. Choose your folder and press Save. When it's done un-binhexing, Quit the File menu.

5. StuffIt has now been decoded and will simply have a ".sea" extension. This means it is a "self-extracting archive." All you have to do to install it is double-click on the StuffIt icon. When the dialog box appears, leave the file name alone and choose to install it on your desktop. Then select Save and you're done.

Unpacking Netscape

Once Netscape has downloaded to your system, it should have unpacked into a new file called Netscape Installer. If for some reason it hasn't, all you have to do is send it over to StuffIt Expander for unpacking. This is as simple as dragging your Netscape Navigator file icon over to the StuffIt icon and dropping it. StuffIt will do the rest.

Installing Netscape

This is the easy part. Find the Netscape Installer icon. Double-click on it. Choose the folder you want Netscape to be installed in. It's a good idea to make a folder called "Netscape" or "Internet" or "WWW," whatever makes sense to you. Then you can put Netscape and all your helper applications into that. Click on Install and Netscape will install itself. That's it. We're ready to go.

One more piece of advice, though. Once you've determined that Netscape is operating fine, in the interest of good housekeeping you might want to trash the Netscape Installer file. You don't need it anymore, and at over 1.5mb it's too big to keep hanging around cluttering up your hard drive.

Getting Set Up

You should be able to start up and begin operating Netscape Navigator immediately. However, be aware that some functions on the menu, such as newsgroups and mail operations, will not work until you first make the appropriate settings.

Setting Basic Preferences

First, go to the Options menu and if the Show Location option is not checked, click on it to check it. This will make the Location window show up on the upper part of your main Netscape screen (below the toolbar) showing the URL address of the current document. Knowing where you are at any time will help you navigate in your early explorations of the Web. You can disable this feature anytime you want a larger viewing window by "unchecking" Show Location.

To set up initial settings for things like mail, newsgroups and helper applications, choose the Options menu item, then Preferences. The pop-up window that appears has eight different categories for things you can set. We'll talk more about some of these later, but here are some helpful initial settings:

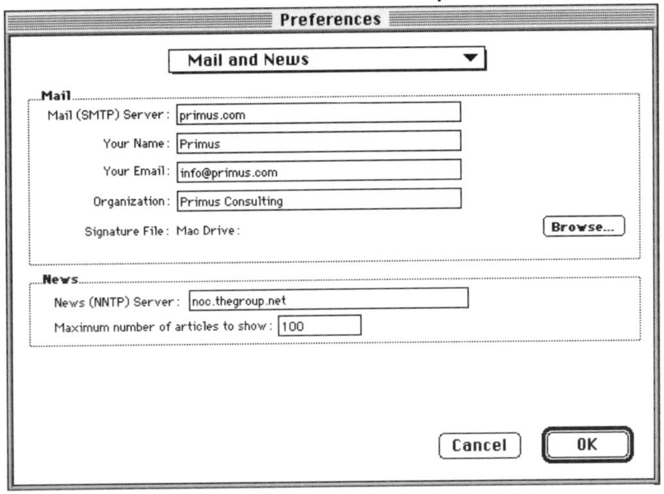

Mail: In the Mail and News dialog box, put in your mail host and your personal e-mail address. If you don't know the name or full pathway of your mail host, ask your sysadmin.

Newsgroups: Put in the name and full pathway of your NNTP newshost in the Mail and News box. It's possible that this is the same as your mail host, but it's not likely. If you don't know it, ask your sysadmin.

TELNET access: If you have software you normally use to access TELNET, go to the Applications and Directories dialog box and use the Browse button to find your TELNET application so that Netscape will know where to find it.

Helper applications: For displaying audio and video files Netscape uses "helper applications." Netscape should already have made note of any helper applications you have and you will see their icons in the pop-up window. Don't worry if you don't have any—you can add them later.

Figure 2-4: One of Netscape's five Preferences dialog boxes.

Note: Netscape Navigator has its own image viewer, which it uses by default to let you view World Wide Web pages without an accessory image viewer, such as JPEGView. With JPEGView the image quality may be somewhat better and you will be able to store and manipulate images in ways that Netscape does not allow. You will not be able to play movie clips without a video application, such as Sparkle. We'll go into helper applications in greater detail in Chapter 4.

Netscape Quick Peek

Ready to set sail on your first cruise of the World Wide Web? Here's what you should have done already:

- Got your local SLIP/PPP connection to the Internet.
- Installed a TCP/IP stack on your system.
- Downloaded and installed Netscape Navigator.

Now, let's go.

First, launch your TCP/IP application. Dial your account and log in. Start Netscape by clicking on the icon.

The first time you run Netscape you will be presented with the license agreement and you'll be asked to accept its terms before continuing. Read, reflect and act accordingly.

As its first act, Netscape will take you to Netscape Communications Corporation's home page (Figure 2-5). As it searches for its connection, you'll see the little logo on the top right side of the screen begin to activate; then you'll see the page-loading information on the bottom of the screen. All of this means that you're already sailing the Net!

Note: If the logo continues to be active and nothing's happening on the bottom of the screen except for a message saying "Trying to locate host...," you've got a connection problem. You may have to talk to your sysadmin or other technical support source to get it straightened out.

Netscape's home page gives you information on the latest developments with Netscape (see Figure 2-5). You'll be given an opportunity to register your copy of Netscape, a good idea if you want to be apprised of updates.

Just above the main screen (your "Web TV") you'll see the directory buttons. Each of these takes you to another information page about

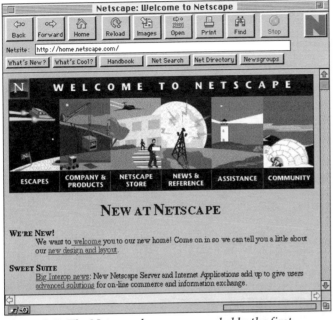

Figure 2-5: The Netscape home page: probably the first Web page you will ever see.

Netscape. One useful button is "Handbook," which takes you to Netscape's online manual. If you've got any problems to solve or questions about setup, this is the place where you're likely to find the answers.

You can follow any links by clicking on the high-lighted words on any page. They'll take you to the next page of information on that topic.

After accessing a page and reading it, you can "back out" of it by choosing the Back button from the toolbar on the top of the screen. This will return you to the previously displayed page. If you're several pages along, you can keep backing out until you get to your original starting point. Netscape keeps a short list of where you've been—a little trail of bread crumbs through the forest, so you can follow your path back. Or choose the Home button on the toolbar and you'll return immediately to the Welcome page—unless you're ahead of the class and have already figured out how to set your own home page.

Using URLs

Now let's go some place exciting and have some fun. Click on Open on the toolbar and a long rectangular Open Location window will pop up. This is like jumping into a taxi in a strange town. Like most taxi drivers, this one expects you to know where you want to go. You must enter an address in the window.

Every Web page has its own address, its URL (Uniform Resource Locator). The window is extra-long because all the addresses on the World Wide Web are long. And, as you'll find out, they must be entered just right.

If you already have the address of a Web site you'd like to check out, you can enter it now. Then click on the Open button and you're on your way. If, like a lot of people who are new in town, you don't know any addresses yet, pick one that interests you from our list at the back of the book, or try ours, as shown in Figure 2-6.

Click on "Open"—*et voilà! Bienvenue au WebMuseum Paris!* You have just docked along the Seine in Paris, France, where you are ready to take a tour of the collection of the Louvre, one of the most famous art museums in the world (see Figure 2-7).

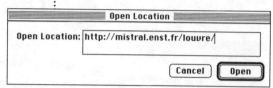

Figure 2-6: The Open Location dialog box: We're off to Paris!

Besides the fun of traveling halfway around the world in a few seconds, this Web site is a good one for illustrating the ways Web pages work. You'll notice a menu of things you can do from this welcome page—including taking a tour of famous paintings in the Louvre, following links to information about various artists, visiting a special exhibit, and taking sightseeing tours of Paris. Choose any one item from this menu by clicking on the highlighted text and you'll go to another page of options.

Many of the pages contain small photos. You'll see colored borders around the pictures, just like the highlighted text links. This means you can click on the pictures and obtain larger versions of them to display on your screen. (The initial pictures are kept deliberately small so that they won't take a long time to load.) If you've got your audio system configured, you can also visit the auditorium and choose a little music to play while you stroll. Ah, Paris!

Wander around Paris with the WebMuseum Paris awhile and soon you'll be feeling like a sophisticated citizen of the Web.

Figure 2-7: This page by Nicholas Pioch (taken before the name change to WebMuseum Paris) has won many design awards—and rightly so.

Plugging Into Your Own Home Page

If you like the WebMuseum Paris, you might like to live here for awhile. In the world of the Web anything is possible. You could choose to make the WebMuseum your home page, so that every time you start up Netscape you'll go straight to Paris.

Practically speaking, this probably isn't a great idea. The WebMuseum's pages are such big files and so rich in images that you've probably noticed it takes a little while for them to load (unless you're lucky enough to be on a high-powered computer system).

But you can set up any page you choose as your home page and you'll probably want to soon. Many access providers have their own home pages with local information for their clients. If yours does, this might be a good place to start. Or you might want to go straight to some useful data page you've found.

To set your home page, choose "Options" from the menu at the top of the screen. From the pull-down menu, choose Preferences for a dialog box with a pop-up window with several options. Scroll to "Styles" (if it's not already displaying that window) and click or return. This dialog box gives you the option of changing things like fonts and display options—you might want to play around with these later.

One of the options asks whether you want to start Netscape with a blank page or a chosen home page location. Choose the Home Page Location radio button, then enter the address of your chosen home page in the window. Click okay and exit. You now have a new home page that will appear every time you start Netscape, or whenever you click on the Home button on the toolbar—until you change it again.

Later we'll show you how to devise your own home page, containing bookmarks to all your favorite sites so you can access them quickly.

Moving On

If you had a little trouble getting your SLIP/PPP connection to work, you're not alone. It seems to be a fact of life that computer communications never work right the first time. Often they need a few rehearsals before they're ready to perform.

By now, though, all that downloading and installation should be behind you and you're home free. We've already introduced you to some of the features of Netscape. Next we'll tour the screen and take you through it menu by menu and button by button.

MENUS, BUTTONS & BARS

Using Netscape Navigator is a breeze, since most operations are self-explanatory. Once you're all up and running, you should have no problem starting to explore the World Wide Web on your own. Everything you really need is built in, so even without any fancy helper applications, you won't need anything extra until you're ready to tackle some gee-whiz, technowizard sites. But because the program has so many extra features, it may take you a while to discover all the things Netscape can do for you.

One of the things you'll notice as you become familiar with Netscape is that there's almost always more than one way to do something. There's a reason: when you become proficient at navigating your way around the Web, you may decide that it would be nice to have a bigger window for viewing documents. You can unclutter your screen and enlarge it by about one quarter by making the toolbar, the directory buttons and the URL location window disappear. Everything you want to do can then be done using the considerably less screen-hogging menu bar—or even the keyboard, if you and your mouse are not inseparable.

We don't advise getting rid of the buttons and bars until you become familiar with all of the functions, however, and for one very good reason. Whenever a toolbar button is available to perform a function (see Figure 3-1), that's the simplest and fastest way to do it. This is less frequently the case with the directory buttons, which are largely introductory with the exception of that handy Newsgroup button. For that reason we'll start our walkaround of the screen with the toolbar, move on to the menu bar and end with the directory buttons. If there is more than one way of doing a particular function, we'll give you the alternatives, including menu items and keyboard commands. The recommended best way will be highlighted with asterisks.

Finally we'll show you how to set up your bookmark list to your best advantage—a tricky task, but we'll do it step by step. Then we'll take a second look at the options available to you under Preferences, so you can customize Netscape to run the way you want it to and get the most from your helper applications for audio and video files.

The Toolbar: Navigating in Netscape

Figure 3-1: *The nine much-used toolbar buttons.*

The toolbar strip is normally quite prominent (those big buttons are great if you're not all that dexterous with the mouse). You can choose the way you want the toolbar button displayed in the Styles dialog box in Preferences (under Options). If you want to gain some screen size, you can make it go away altogether by unchecking the Show Toolbar option in the Options pull-down menu.

Back

Takes you back to the last Web page you were viewing. The page will almost always come from your cache, and so will load very quickly. If you are on the first page of the session, or at the beginning of your history list, this button and the menu option are both grayed out.

Other Ways of Doing This
Menu Go/Back or ⌘[

Forward

Takes you one page forward in the history list (the record of your recent travels that Netscape keeps for you; see Figures 3-10 and 3-11 and the explanation under Go/History in the menu bar section). Obviously this has no meaning unless you have already done at least one Back move. Like Back, the page comes from your cache and will load quickly, and if you are at the end of your history list the button will be grayed out.

Other Ways of Doing This
Menu Go/Forward or ⌘]

Home

Takes you immediately to your home page. At first the default will be the Netscape Welcome screen. Define whatever home page you want in the Styles dialog box in Preferences (under Options in the Main menu).

Other Ways of Doing This
Menu Go/Home

Reload

At times of heavy-duty use of Netscape, or any other Web browser, you may find curious things happening to your pages. Typefaces will break up; in-line .GIFs will go all crumbly; text will go into "greek" or get partly overlaid by pictures. See Figure 3-2. These are signs that whatever arrangements your computer has for caching are overloaded, and now is when you need the Reload feature. It basically says "This page is a dog's breakfast—let's start over."

Other Ways of Doing This
Menu View/Reload or ⌘R

One other situation in which you might use this feature is when you are trying to view the source code of a page. If the page is coming from your cache, the source code will not be accessible. You will get an error message, and Reload will solve the problem.

Images

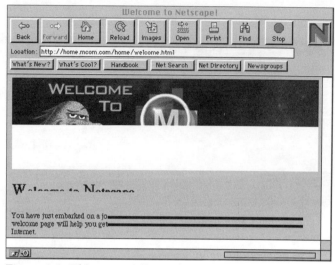

Figure 3-2: *This page really needs to start over: a job for the Reload button.*

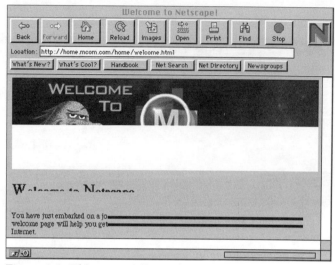 Unless you have lots of computer power at your command (and time to kill), it's a good idea to run Netscape in the "no in-line images" mode on a day-to-day basis (uncheck Auto Load Images on the Options pull-down). It saves time downloading those page decorations that may not add a whole lot. But even the most hurried Web explorer occasionally wants (or needs) to see what the page designer intended.

So, take this option and Netscape redraws the exact same page that's already onscreen, but this time showing all the in-line images.

Open

This is what you do if you know exactly what URL you want to go to but it isn't yet in your bookmark list for handy fly-by-mouse. There's a first time for everything.

A dialog box appears, with a nice L-O-O-O-OOO-ONG window for you to input the URL. Even if your URL reaches the end of the box, you can still keep on entering. Be aware that URL addresses are case-sensitive and have to be entered exactly. Option buttons are Open to tell Netscape to go where you just told it (Enter also works) and Cancel if you think better of it. The key combination W also acts as Cancel.

Other Ways of Doing This:
Menu View/Load Images or ⌘I

Other Ways of Doing This:
Menu File/Open Location or ⌘L

Print

Choosing this brings up the print window, enabling you to change your printer setup or just go ahead and print. The page will print more or less as it looks—not as a source document. (If you want to print source code, use File Save, then get the file into SimpleText and use its print function.)

Other Ways of Doing This
Menu File/Print or ⌘P

Find

Lets you find a word or string in the current document. Don't confuse this with searching the Web for topics. What it does do is let you search a document you've accessed for a particular string—say "sea turtles" in a document on endangered species. You can make the search case-sensitive if you like.

Other Ways of Doing This
Menu Edit/Find or ⌘F

Stop

As long as the stop button is showing red, aborts an attempted connection or loading of a document—usually used because it's taking too long. If you've already accessed the site, it may leave you with a partially loaded page that can be viewed and used normally so far as it goes. At the bottom of the partial page, Netscape thoughtfully adds the reminder "Transfer interrupted!"

Other Ways of Doing This
Menu Go/Stop Loading
ESC
⌘.

Mosaic Users Note: Clicking on the animated logo—the manner of stopping a load in Mosaic—won't work. Instead of stopping a load, it takes you to the Netscape Communications Corporation home page.

Main Menu Bar

| | File | Edit | View | Go | Bookmarks | Options | Directory | Help |

Figure 3-3: *Netscape's eight-item menu bar.*

File

New Window   ⌘N

Select this option and you get a whole new Netscape to play with. This is a very neat feature, taking advantage of the bandwidth of a SLIP connection to bring you multitasking. Say you start Netscape off pulling down a page that you know is going to take time. Instead of drumming your fingers and whistling ten bars of "The Yellow Rose of Texas," you could open another window and do something else. It's also useful if you want to follow a link but keep the original page up at the same time.

The maximum number of windows you can open is set by your entry in the Cache and Network dialog box in Preferences (under Options). Four is a reasonable number—six would be getting greedy (and impossibly slow, on most systems).

Open Location...   ⌘L

Brings up the long dialog box for you to enter the URL address of a Web page you want to go to.

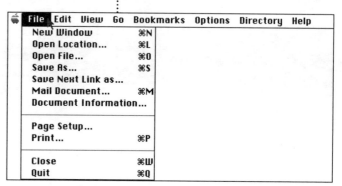

Figure 3-4: *The eleven options in the File pull-down menu.*

Other Ways of Doing This
The toolbar Open button.
Direct entry or drag-and-drop into the URL window.

Figure 3-5: *Netscape lets you do four things at once, if you're so inclined.*

Open File... ⌘O

This option is very different from the Open Location option. This option brings an HTML file from your own computer (or local network) into Netscape where it will be interpreted as a Web page. This is the so-called "local mode" used all the time by Web page authors using Netscape as an authoring tool when writing files in HTML (HyperText Markup Language). We'll be explaining HTML in Chapter 5 of this book.

Save As... ⌘S

This is how to save a Web document that you want to preserve, manipulate, send someone for Christmas, plagiarize or feed to your dog.

You may have a decision to make during this process. The current document can be saved either as "text," meaning that the embedded HTML stuff like <P> and <DL> will be eliminated, or as "Source," meaning that the <P>s and <DL>s will be preserved. Your decision on this depends on how you want to use the file. Since it's the HTML codes that create the look of the page, if you save a file as Source you will be able to recall it to Netscape at any time as a local file using the Open File option. If, on the other hand, you want to use the saved file in, say, your word processor, then you can take the default of "Text" and it will look as near as possible the same as it did onscreen.

Since this is the Web, what you are saving may not be text at all—it may be a picture, a sound, a movie. Netscape will save these files in the appropriate format.

Save Next Link As...

This is not really a menu option (although it was in some earlier versions of the software) but it's a useful feature and this seems a good place to explain it. Netscape lets you save a page to a file without actually displaying it at all. This could be quite a time-saver if it's a complex document and the Net is being crabby, as it often is (especially on Fridays when every university computer comes up for weekly maintenance). Place your cursor on the hypertext link to the page, then hold down the Option key as you click the mouse button. You will be led straight to the Save As... dialog box, and Netscape should be clever enough to know whether you are saving text, a picture, a movie or audio.

Mail Document...   ⌘M

This might well have been put on a different menu or button and just called Netscape's "outgoing mail" feature, for that's really what it is, and a very nice one too.

When you select "Mail Document," a large dialog box appears which is basically an e-mail blank ready for you to fill out. The Subject box defaults to the name of your current document. The Quote Document button allows you to add the text of the current document. You can also attach another file you have on hand with the Attach button. But you can easily ignore all that and simply send a general message (for instance, to send comments to a Web page author).

If you *do* want to include the text of your current page, you'll find that a piece of cake too. Simply click on the Quote Document button, and the text is imported into the message body window in a flash. Each line starts with the > symbol, like a conventional e-mail quote. (See Figure 3-6.) Also, all of the HTML

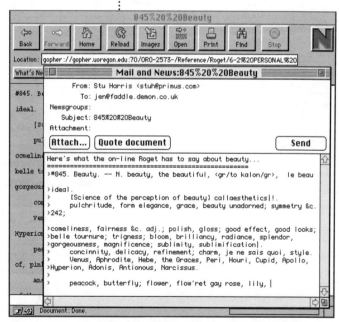

Figure 3-6: *An entry from the online thesaurus turned into e-mail in a flash.*

codes are edited out. There's no perfect way to do this, but the other neat thing about this feature is that you can put a cursor in there and edit away to your heart's content.

When you're done, there's a big button to send your mail on its way.

HOT TIP

You can also drop into the message body anything in the Clipboard—an extract from a Web page that you've previously outlined and done "Edit Copy" (⌘C) with, for instance. Simply place your cursor where you want the text and press ⌘V.

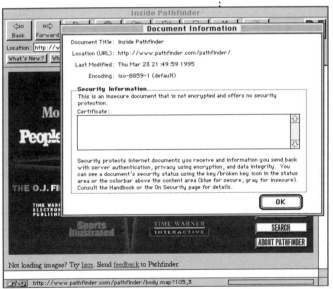

Figure 3-7: *The Document Information box tells you about security.*

Warning: Your message is going nowhere if you have not told Netscape about your e-mail arrangements in Preferences: Mail and News.

Document Information...

Choosing this item brings up the document information box (see Figure 3-7), giving information about the history and security of the current page.

Page Setup...

This allows you to change your page setup for printing—change paper size, switch fonts, reduce or enlarge the document, and change the page orientation (revolve the image).

☾ HOT TIP —·—·—·—·—·—·—·—·—·—·—·—·—·—·—·—·—

Printing will often cut off the right margin if the window is larger than the page. You can scale down the size to 90 percent or whatever's necessary in Page Setup to print the full page.

Print ⌘P

Same as the Print button on the toolbar. Brings up the print window, enabling you to change your printer setup or just go ahead and print. You can also save to a PostScript file.

Close ⌘W

Closes the Netscape window. If you have more than one Netscape window running (see "New Window"), that may not be the end of Netscape. You'll have to close down the other windows, natch.

Quit ⌘Q

This is the end of Netscape, regardless of how many Netscapes you had running.

Edit

You won't be using these features very much—in normal operations they are all grayed out, with the exceptions of Copy and Find, and even the Find feature is more conveniently invoked with the toolbar Find button.

You can, however, outline any text in the Netscape content window, no matter what size or type style,

Other Ways of Doing This
***The toolbar Print button

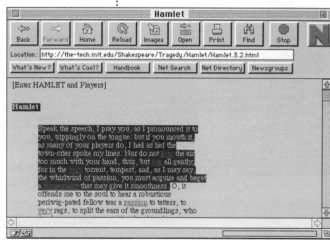

Figure 3-8: *Part of a speech from Hamlet, Act III Scene 2, about to go onto the Clipboard.*

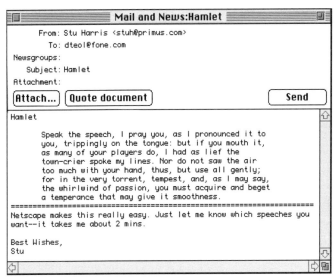

```
┌─────────────────────────────────────────────┐
│ ▤▤  ═══════ Mail and News:Hamlet ═══════  ▤ │
├─────────────────────────────────────────────┤
│     From: Stu Harris <stuh@primus.com>        │
│       To: dteol@fone.com                      │
│ Newsgroups:                                   │
│   Subject: Hamlet                             │
│ Attachment:                                   │
│ ┌────────┐┌───────────────┐      ┌──────────┐│
│ │Attach..││Quote document │      │   Send   ││
│ └────────┘└───────────────┘      └──────────┘│
│ Hamlet                                     ⬆ │
│                                               │
│      Speak the speech, I pray you, as I pronounced it to │
│      you, trippingly on the tongue: but if you mouth it, │
│      as many of your players do, I had as lief the       │
│      town-crier spoke my lines. Nor do not saw the air   │
│      too much with your hand, thus, but use all gently;  │
│      for in the very torrent, tempest, and, as I may say,│
│      the whirlwind of passion, you must acquire and beget│
│      a temperance that may give it smoothness.           │
│ ================================================         │
│ Netscape makes this really easy. Just let me know which speeches you │
│ want--it takes me about 2 mins.                          │
│                                                          │
│ Best Wishes,                                             │
│ Stu                                        ⬇ │
│ ◁                                         ▷ ▱│
└─────────────────────────────────────────────┘
```

Figure 3-9: *Hamlet by e-mail. What would the Bard think of this?*

and use Copy to place it on the Clipboard. At any time during the same session, you can drop this text fragment into any other application having Copy/Cut/Paste features: a SimpleText document or an e-mail message, for instance.

These Undo/Cut/Copy/Paste/Find edit functions really come into their own, however, when you are entering text into a WWW form or creating Netscape e-mail. (See Figures 3-8 and 3-9.)

⟳ HOT TIP ─ ▪ ─ ▪ ─ ▪ ─ ▪ ─ ▪ ─ ▪ ─ ▪

If the extract you'd like to copy is too long to fit on one screen, Netscape has a handy feature to help you out. Outline text of any length as follows: Click on the first word of the extract, and you should see a "selection marker" appear. Now scroll to the end of the extract and hold down the Shift key as you click again.

─ ▪ ─ ▪ ─ ▪ ─ ▪ ─ ▪ ─ ▪ ─ ▪ ─ ▪

View

Reload ⌘R

Same as the toolbar Reload button. Remakes the same page you are currently viewing. Use if the image being loaded from cache has deteriorated.

Load Images ⌘I

Used when you are running Netscape in "No in-line images" mode. Reloads the page adding the images.

Other Ways of Doing This
***The toolbar Reload button

Other Ways of Doing This
***The toolbar Images button

Source...

Well, we've mentioned the "source document" and the "source code" a few times already. This is how you see the source—it just means the page as originally coded in the HTML convention by its author. HTML enthusiasts—and that includes us—love this feature because it enables us to go to all the best-looking pages in the world and crib off their authors' work. The Web is a free-for-all that makes copyright attorneys wake up screaming in the night.

Go

The Web is so endlessly fascinating that you are very likely to go wandering off across the world for hours, especially if you're using a Web Crawler to look up keywords. It would take a photographic memory to remember how on earth you got to where you are now. Netscape remembers for you—it keeps track of where you go and allows you to call up the history list at any time. The history list, like a trail of bread crumbs in the forest, is what enables you to retrace your steps safely. Generally these will be in your cache.

You can return to a previous page in your history list simply by clicking on it in the list and it will be reloaded from the cache. You can also go back or forward one page at a time. The Go pull-down menu, as seen in Figure 3-10, is almost entirely concerned with navigating the history list in both directions.

Back   ⌘[

Same as the Back button on the toolbar. Takes you back to the last Web page you were viewing. If you are on the first page of the session, or at the beginning of your history list, this menu option and the toolbar button are both grayed out.

Other Ways of Doing This
***The toolbar Back button

Other Ways of Doing This
***The toolbar Forward button

Other Ways of Doing This
***The toolbar Home button

Other Ways of Doing This
***The toolbar Stop button

Forward ⌘]

Takes you one page forward in the history list. Obviously this has no meaning unless you have already done at least one Back move.

Home

Takes you immediately to your home page (as defined by you in the Styles dialog box in Preferences (under Options).

Stop Loading ⌘.

Aborts loading of a document—usually used because loading is taking too long. Leaves you with a partially loaded page that can be viewed and used normally so far as it goes.

View History... ⌘H

Tacked on beneath the five Go menu options is an abbreviated version of the history list itself (see Figure 3-10). You can go to any page in the list simply by clicking on that page's title in the list. You can also go to any of the last ten pages you visited by using ⌘0 through ⌘9 (choose the number next to the page you want).

For a more detailed look at the history list you can click on View History. This nice wide window (Figure 3-11), horizontally scrollable, fits those very long URL addresses that overflow the main URL window. The most recently loaded pages are at the top. Option buttons are Go To, and Add To Bookmarks. Double-clicking anywhere in the list reloads that page.

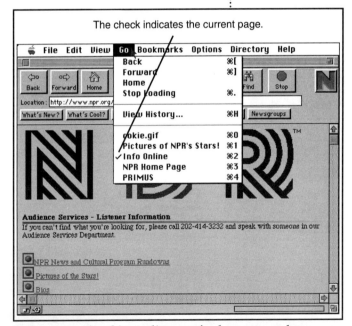

Figure 3-10: *Our history list as we've begun to explore National Public Radio's Web pages.*

Bookmarks

As you cruise the Net, you can use the Add Bookmark option to create a list of pages you might want
to revisit. Once you begin to create bookmarks, a list
of your bookmark pages or bookmark categories will
appear here. You can go to any bookmarked page
immediately by clicking on it in this list.

Creating and managing a proper hierarchy of
bookmarks is a task we'll tackle in "How to Use
Bookmarks" later in this chapter.

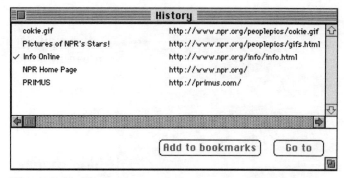

Figure 3-11: *The generous window you get when you ask for View History.*

Add bookmark   ⌘D

Click here to add the current page to your bookmark list. If you have
already set up bookmark categories it will be added to whatever hierarchy you have specified in the Edit Bookmarks screen (the default is the
top level of listings).

View bookmarks...   ⌘B

Choose this option and you get an extended view of your bookmark
list with editing options (see the section on "How to Use Bookmarks").

Options

Preferences...

This menu option leads to a set of eight dialog boxes that set up and
customize your Netscape. We covered some initial setups in Chapter 2
and will be dealing with Preferences later in this chapter under Setting
Special Preferences.

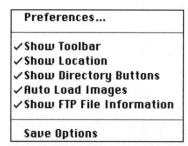

Figure 3-12: *Five toggle-check features in the Options pull-down menu.*

Show Toolbar

Check to show the toolbar. Uncheck to remove the toolbar from your screen.

Show Location

If this option is checked, you get a URL window below the toolbar showing the location (the URL address) of the current document. When unchecked, it goes away.

Show Directory Buttons

If unchecked, the directory buttons disappear, giving you a larger screen area—probably one of the first things you'll want to get rid of.

Auto Load Images

As we pointed out before, it saves lots of download time to run Netscape routinely with this option unchecked—i.e., not displaying those in-line .GIFs. However, certain Web pages make very little sense without the in-lines (see Figure 3-13)—and you won't be able to tell the difference between a picture and a sound bite.

Show FTP File Information

When you access anonymous FTP sites with Netscape, you get a description of contents in the available files with update notes or whatever. Uncheck this item and the file information disappears, allowing more files to be displayed on the screen.

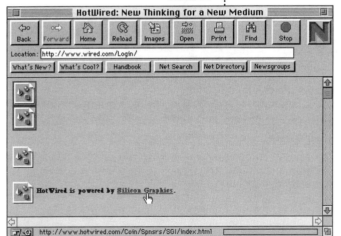

Figure 3-13: *The icon that Netscape uses to indicate a missing in-line image—and a Web page that makes no sense without the images.*

Save Options

The way you set up your toggle checklist will be temporary, applying to this Netscape session only, unless you select the Save Options box. Preferences are saved automatically.

Directory

All but one of the options in the Directory pull-down menu takes you straight to Netscape Communications Corporation where Web pages are posted to give you help and information in your explorations of the Web. (The one exception is Go To Newsgroups.) Many of these menu options duplicate functions of Directory buttons. Most are self-explanatory.

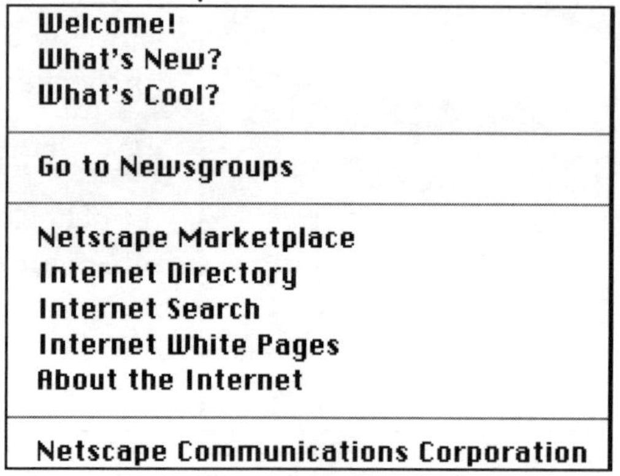

Netscape's Home

This is the "Home Page" Netscape sets up for you by default to get you going. Netscape Communications Corporation's home page is the place to go to find out about any new releases or the latest development in the software.

What's New?

Same as the What's New? directory button. This is an archived monthly update of new Internet resources—with links to the latest Web pages online.

What's Cool?

Same as the What's Cool? directory button. This is a collection of favorite Web pages by "the Supreme Arbiter of Taste" at Netscape Communications Corporation.

| Welcome! |
| What's New? |
| What's Cool? |
| Go to Newsgroups |
| Netscape Marketplace |
| Internet Directory |
| Internet Search |
| Internet White Pages |
| About the Internet |
| Netscape Communications Corporation |

Figure 3-14: *The Directory pull-down menu.*

Go to Newsgroups

This is how you access USENET newsgroups. For a description of Netscape's fine newsreader, see Chapter 4 of this book.

Netscape Galleria

Netscape Communications Corporation maintains this page as a gallery of online services and content offerings from customers of their Netsite Communications Server and Netsite Commerce Server.

Netsite server customers can request a listing on this page by e-mailing to: marketplace@netscape.com.

Internet Directory

Same as the Net Directory directory button. This is a hyperlinked list of directories you can access to find things on the Internet. You can search for subjects, commercial services and business sites, and find a directory of servers here.

Internet Search

Same as the Net Search directory button. Links to various "search engines" as they're called. You can search document titles or content by WebCrawler, Lycos, etc. More on this in Chapter 6.

Internet White Pages

Trying to find someone on the Net? Use the services listed here to locate a person or organization. Several Gopher and TELNET sites collect the e-mail addresses and names of users on the Internet which can be accessed by different search means here.

About the Internet

If you're ready to study up a little further, you'll find more useful information about the Net in general here. Cocktail party experts can crib from excerpts from *The Whole Internet User's Guide* and *Big Dummy's Guide to the Internet*, with the lowdown on the history of the Net. Follow other links to FAQs and online guides.

Help

About Netscape

This is a copyright notice. (The lawyers advised them to put this page in.)

Handbook

Access to Netscape's online manual—a pretty complete reference guide to setting up and operating Netscape (though not as friendly as this book).

Release Notes

Tells you which version of Netscape you are running, with release notes concerning problems and fixes recently implemented. If you're having problems with some of your setups, you might check here.

Frequently Asked Questions

Besides answering basic questions, it's a useful guide to common problems users may encounter. Look here first before badgering your sysadmin.

On Security

An exhaustive explanation of how Netscape (in collaboration with RSA Data Security Inc.) handles encryption of secure pages. If that's not exhaustive enough, there are three hypertext links you can follow. We'd like to tell you where the links lead, but it's hush-hush.

How to Give Feedback

Instructions on how to tell the Netscape designers what you think of their product, and how to report bugs you think you may have found.

How to Get Support

Info here for business clients who want to use Netscape on a commercial scale and want to arrange for support services.

How to Create Web Services

If you're curious about how to create your own Web documents, go to this directory for references to documents that will tell you how to write WWW documents and direct you to HTML learning and style guides.

Directory Buttons

The directory buttons are largely a convenience for new users—useful while you're getting acquainted but quickly outgrown. Everything on

Figure 3-15: *The six directory buttons.*

them is duplicated in the menu bar, under either Directory or Help. When you're ready to do away with them, uncheck Show Directory Buttons under Options and you'll gain a centimeter or so of page space.

What's New?	Same as menu bar Directory/What's New?
What's Cool?	Same as menu bar Directory/What's Cool?
Handbook	Same as menu bar Help/Handbook.
Net Search	Same as menu bar Directory/Internet Search.
Net Directory	Same as menu bar Directory/Internet Directory.
Newsgroups	Same as Directory/Go to Newsgroups

Mouse tricks

There's one more useful button to describe, and it isn't on the screen at all. It's the one you often find under your finger. Yes, that one—the mouse button. Along about Version 1.1 beta 1, somebody in the Netscape dream factory had a bright idea about how to make special use of it. Hold it down for two seconds when pointing to a link or an in-line .GIF, and up pops a very useful menu offering things you might like to do.

If you're on a hyperlink, you get these options:

• Go Back or Forward in your history list.

• Open this Link

• Add Bookmark for this Link

• New Window with this Link

• Save this Link as...

• Copy this Link Location (meaning "place its URL on the Clipboard")

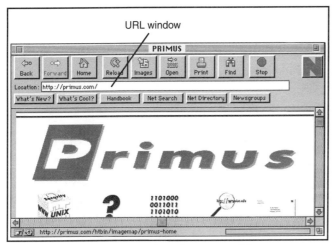

Figure 3-16: *The URL window shows you either where you are or where you're headed.*

Other Ways of Doing This
***The OPEN toolbar button
Menu File/Open Location

If you're pointing at an image, these are your choices:

- View this Image
- Save this Image as...
- Copy this Image (meaning "place the image itself on the Clipboard")
- Copy this Image Location (meaning "place its URL on the Clipboard")
- Load this Image (use this when you're in "No images" mode to inspect one specific image)

That second option, "Save Image As...", is a terrific time-saver. Towards the end of Chapter 5 we'll show you how to use it to perform acts of cyberlarceny that used to take quite some figuring out, and that pop-up menu is shown in Figure 5-10. Also on this mini-menu are shortcuts to Back and Forward.

Activity & Location Indicators

The URL Window

Put a cursor in here with your mouse and enter a URL. Netscape will go to that address as soon as you Enter.

If you've about had it with typing "http://", the good news is you needn't bother any more. Both this URL window and the one that pops up when you hit the toolbar Open button will assume you mean http:// unless you actually specify some other protocol, such as ftp://.

Both these windows are the same size—60 characters—so neither has any advantage for long URLs. But note that while the visible URL window will always be displaying the current page, the toolbar Open window sticks with whatever you last entered in it. You can save a lot of keystrokes by making just the minimum changes to an existing URL in order to go off somewhere else, so we recommend that you use the toolbar Open window when starting off for a completely new destination (unless it's in your bookmark list, of course). The visible window will follow whatever links you do, and that way you'll have two possible URL addresses to use a a basis for minor editing.

⟲ HOT TIP

If a long and complicated URL fails, try removing everything after the basic host name plus just one slash. Then if you can get through to the host, use the URL window to add back the rest of the address, bit by bit. Or the host may offer you a link to where you want to go. It's possible the directory structure has changed or was not noted correctly.

Title bar

The title bar is the strip at the very top of the screen between the main window buttons (Figure 3-17). When you go to a new Web page, anything that the page's author designated as "<TITLE>" in the HTML code ends up in this strip. It's usually the first part of the document to arrive, and so serves as the first indication that you've come to the right place (like the first swallow arriving at San Juan Capistrano in spring).

Some titles may be so long, or your window so narrow, that they overflow. In this case the title is truncated from the right. URLs can become exceedingly long, and the only place you can be sure of seeing them absolutely complete is in the box you get by selecting Go/View History from the Menu bar.

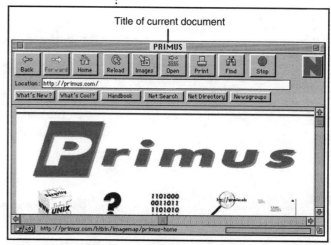

Figure 3-17: *What appears in your title bar is under the control of the page's author.*

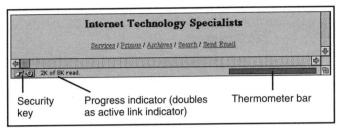

Figure 3-18: *The various components of the Netscape progress bar.*

Progress Bar

Way down at the bottom of your Netscape window is a little strip known as the progress bar. Actually, it's two separate bars, both of which inform you about progress in loading a Web page—or a component such as a picture, movie or sound bite. It's certainly nice to be able to look down and see "22% of 107K read" and then "Document Done." The thermometer bar is a comfort too, just to let you know that something's happening—but its accuracy is a bit hand-waving. It has an annoying habit of pausing just as it seems to be almost done.

The large progress bar also displays the URL of any active link your mouse cursor is pointing at, including the name of an external image. It can be very useful to know where you will be taken if you click on that link. It's also used to give you a one-liner about any pull-down menu item you may be pointing at.

Security Key

Security was one of the principal concerns of the Internet when it was first set up as a military Net in the '60s. For more than a decade now, security has taken a back seat as the Net has become a DMZ. But now, as more and more merchants are using the Web to display their wares, offering potential clients the convenience of ordering by credit card, security is once again a concern.

It is now possible to produce "secure" Web pages—meaning that the text is encrypted during transmission to you, and, even more important, that any information you enter into a form is encrypted before it leaves you. For more on this, read the essay under Help/On Security in the main menu. You won't find many of these yet, but when you do, Netscape will signal you. The broken key icon at the extreme lower left will change to an unbroken key and the blue security colorbar will appear at the top of the screen between the directory buttons and the content window. If you want to see what this looks like, go to any of the Netscape Communications Corporation's pages on your Directory or Help menus, such as Welcome, then add an "s" to change the address in your URL window to begin "https://" and return.

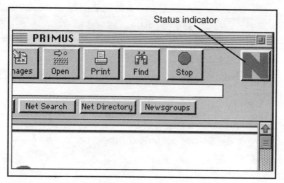

Figure 3-19: *We call this the logo but its official name is the status indicator.*

Status Indicator (Logo)

Animates during loading and while searching for a host.

How to Use Bookmarks

Managing bookmark lists for graphical Web browsers is definitely a hang-up. The problem is that we can all imagine what our ideal bookmark manager should be like, but for an application programmer to provide the tools you need to get from here to there is quite another matter. The bookmark features of Netscape's beta (prerelease) versions were pretty rough, and you were on your own in figuring out how to make them work. Fortunately, there has been substantial improvement, but figuring out how it all works is not as straightforward as you might hope.

It may help at the outset to realize that all of your bookmark information is contained in a file called BOOKMARKS. Take a look at it with the Open File command on your File menu. Aha! Yes, as you make up your bookmark list you are actually creating a hypertext document.

So be patient; don't expect the computer to intuit your intentions, and before very long you'll end up with the hierarchical bookmark list of your dreams.

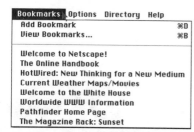

Figure 3-20: *Our first few bookmarks.*

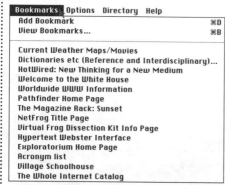

Figure 3-21: *At this point we knew our bookmark list needed organizing.*

Creating Your First Few Bookmarks

Opinions may vary about this, but our advice is to just add your first few bookmarks in haphazard fashion by going to a page you like and using the main menu option Bookmarks/Add bookmark (or ⌘D). The process happens so quickly that you won't see any evidence of your new bookmark until you highlight Bookmarks in the menu bar. (See Figures 3-20 and 3-21.) Then there it is, its title appended below the pull-down menu. Move the mouse to the bookmark, and you'll go right to that page.

As you add more and more of your pet pages, you'll begin to understand the need for managing the list more logically. It doesn't take too many pet pages to overflow the screen height and make that list unusable.

Categorizing Bookmark Lists

The first step is to move your bookmarks around so that they are grouped in categories. Think about the categories that would be useful to you personally. In the list shown here, some obvious categories would be Reference, Educational and Magazines. The rest can be grouped as General for now.

The bookmark editing window comes in two versions, depending on how many options you want displayed. For our purposes, we'll treat them as the elementary and advanced windows. Get the elementary window up using Bookmarks/View bookmarks (or ⌘B) in the main menu. It should look like Figure 3-22. (If you get the larger screen shown in Figure 3-23, you can click on Fewer Options to get the reduced screen.)

Now you can use the mouse to highlight any bookmark in the list, making it the "current" bookmark. A double-click, or a click on the Go To button sends Netscape off to that particular bookmarked page. Notice that the Up/Dn/PgUp/PgDn/Home/End keys on your keyboard, as well as the

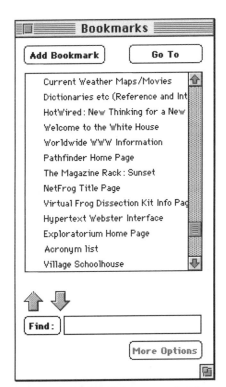

Figure 3-22: *The "elementary" side of the bookmark window.*

scroll bars, navigate the list. Next, get used to the idea that you can move the current bookmark around the list using the up and down arrows. It's easy: pretty soon you'll have all your bookmarks grouped appropriately.

Adding Headers & Separators

What we're working toward is having a pull-down bookmark menu that includes "Reference," "Educational," "Magazines," and whatever else we choose, so that highlighting Magazines produces the Magazine list to pick from, and so on. That's what is meant by a hierarchical list, and we're not there yet.

To get there, you need to graduate to the "advanced" window. Do this by clicking on the More Options button at the extreme lower right.

Now as you cruise your list, you can see some of the extra information that Netscape stores for you on each item in the list: its URL address, obviously, but also the date/time you created it and last visited it. There's also a generous-sized window in which you can write a mini-essay singing the praises of this page. Note that although this window does not have Edit Cut/Copy/Paste options of its own, anything on the edit Clipboard (such as text you outlined in the page itself) can be dropped into this space using ⌘V.

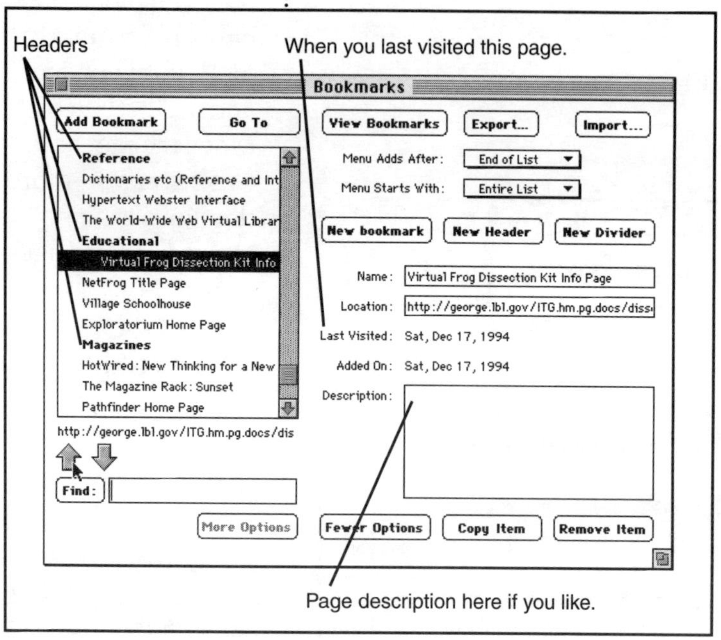

By far the most interesting button is the one labeled New Header. When you use it, the header will pop in immediately below the current list item. So position the list selector just above one of your category groupings, press New Header and enter the category label in the Name window. Then click on the New Header label in your book-

Headers

When you last visited this page.

Bookmarks

| Add Bookmark | Go To | | View Bookmarks | Export... | Import... |

Reference
Dictionaries etc (Reference and Int
Hypertext Webster Interface
The World-Wide Web Virtual Librar
Educational
Virtual Frog Dissection Kit Info
NetFrog Title Page
Village Schoolhouse
Exploratorium Home Page
Magazines
HotWired: New Thinking for a New
The Magazine Rack: Sunset
Pathfinder Home Page

http://george.lb1.gov/ITG.hm.pg.docs/dis

Find:

Menu Adds After: End of List
Menu Starts With: Entire List

New bookmark   New Header   New Divider

Name: Virtual Frog Dissection Kit Info Page
Location: http://george.lb1.gov/ITG.hm.pg.docs/diss
Last Visited: Sat, Dec 17, 1994
Added On: Sat, Dec 17, 1994
Description:

More Options   Fewer Options   Copy Item   Remove Item

Page description here if you like.

Figure 3-23: *A click on the up arrow indents the Virtual Frog, making it part of the Educational bookmark list.*

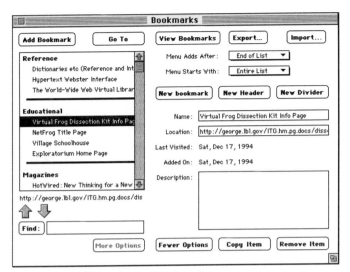

Figure 3-24: *Everything shipshape?*

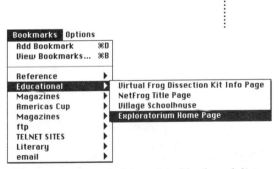

Figure 3-25: *A truly hierarchical bookmark list at last.*

mark list. Your header now appears in the main list in the appropriate place in bold.

Now it's a matter of telling Netscape that the items below the header belong to that category. It's not automatically assumed. Items below the header must be *indented* to become part of that category. Here the Netscape coders have elected to make this an extra function of the up and down arrows rather than a separate function. Here's how it works:

You'll find that an item will move up the list using the up arrow, but when you push it up against a Header or an indented item, it indents instead of moving. (Conversely, moving an indented item with the down arrow cancels indentation when it hits a non-indented line.) So, in Figure 3-23 moving Virtual Frog Dissection Kit "up" will indent it and make it belong to the Educational category. Start with the first item under each header, then click on the up arrow and it will indent. Move down to the next item and repeat until all the items under the header are indented.

Repeat that process for all your categories. Then use the New Divider button to add a line between categories and make the list even clearer. It finishes off the list as shown in Figure 3-24 and has the desired result on your main screen's pull-down menus, shown in Figure 3-25.

Going back to the bookmark edit screen, you'll discover that if you make a Header the current item, pressing the up or down arrow moves the Header together with its entire indented sublist. Also, pressing Remove Item, which would normally just delete a redundant bookmark, now deletes the whole sublist. (Netscape has the grace to warn you and ask for confirmation before going ahead.)

Now, if you feel like getting really clever some rainy day, prove to yourself that you can set up second-level headers (double-indented), then third-, fourth-, fifth-level headers to make a superlist.

⊘ HOT TIP ── ∙ ── ∙ ── ∙ ── ∙ ── ∙ ── ∙ ── ∙ ──

If you have a particularly complex bookmark list, make a backup copy of the BOOKMARKS file. Otherwise, a disk crash could wipe out all of your list-management work.

── ∙ ── ∙ ── ∙ ── ∙ ── ∙ ── ∙ ── ∙ ── ∙ ──

Other Bookmark Options

Now that you have a decently ordered list, you can make use of a couple of other Netscape bookmark-management features.

Use the pop-up menu labeled Menu Starts With to tell Netscape to show you listings in only one of your categories as opposed to the Entire List (which means just your top-level Headers). Use Menu Adds After to tell Netscape that until further notice any bookmarks you add belong in the Reference category (or whatever).

If your bookmark list gets very complicated and you'd like to see a simplified version of it in the bookmark edit window, you can make all bookmarks that belong under a header disappear by double-clicking on the header. The header will appear underlined to remind you of the unseen bookmarks, and they can be brought back again any time you like by double-clicking on the same header again.

Making Your Bookmark List Your Home Page
Since your bookmark list is an actual Web document, it's possible to make that your home page and make accessing your favorite pages easy. Doing so is slightly tricky, however. This is how:

1. Go to the Bookmarks editing window (Bookmarks/View Bookmarks, then click on More Options for the full screen).

2. Click on View Bookmarks. Your hypertext Bookmarks page will appear in the main screen.

3. Return to the main screen and note the URL in the Location window.

4. Go to the Styles dialog box in Preferences (under Options).

5. In the Home Page Location box enter the URL you noted, which is the location of your BOOKMARKS file. (If it's very long, you can use the edit copy command to copy it into the Home Page Location window.)

Return to the main screen. When you click on Home it should go to your new bookmarks home page.

Figure 3-26: *Our bookmark list turned into a personal Web page.*

Turning Your Bookmark List Into a Web Page

Don't forget, your bookmark list is actually a hypertext document. To prove it, use the View Bookmarks button, then close this window (Escape will do as well as the Close button) and behold your list looking just like a Web page! (See Figure 3-26.)

For the title, it uses the name you provided in the Mail and News dialog box in Preferences (under Options). You can use it as you would any Web page, following the hypertext links to your bookmarked pages. Every time you change your bookmark list, you should use View Bookmarks to save your changes to your BOOKMARKS file.

Exporting & Importing Bookmarks

These options simply allow you to save the list under any name (Export) or add another bookmark file to your current bookmark file (Import). Obviously, these options also offer a way of managing several alternative bookmark lists or trading bookmark files with other users.

Multiple users can create their own bookmark files by using the Export command and giving the file a different name than the default BOOKMARKS. A separate Netscape icon will be created and you can launch Netscape with your alternate bookmark list by clicking on the appropriate icon. Another way of doing this, which allows you to change other Preferences as well, is covered in "Customizing Netscape for Multiple Users" later in this chapter.

Setting Special Preferences

No doubt once you get familiar with Netscape you'll want to customize it for your own use, perhaps configuring the screen to look the way
you want or adding new helper applications you collect on your Web
cruises. Some Preferences you have already set just to get Netscape
running properly. Other settings are at the tip of your mouse finger
whenever you want them.

Choose Preferences under the Options pull-down menu. The pop-up
menu at the head of the Preferences dialog box lets you determine
whether the box is going to be concerned with Styles; Fonts and Colors;
Mail and News; Cache and Network; Applications and Directories;
Images and Security; Proxies; or Helper Applications.

Window & Link Styles

You can customize the appearance of your screen in the Styles
box. Radio buttons allow you to select the appearance of the
toolbar, and an input window is available for you to set the
URL of your home page or to have Netscape start with just a
blank page. This is important: the default is the Netscape Welcome page, and after you've seen that a few times you'll want
to select something else. Once you've got your bookmarks all
nicely organized you might want to make your BOOKMARKS
file your default home page (see the sidebar in the previous
section on how to do this). In addition, you can select the font
you want for the text on your page.

In the Link Styles box you can customize the colors Netscape
uses for links, and a checkbox allows you to decide whether
you want links underlined. Links are the hypertext words that
appear by default in blue and underlined on your screen, letting
you know that a different page can be accessed by clicking on the ap-

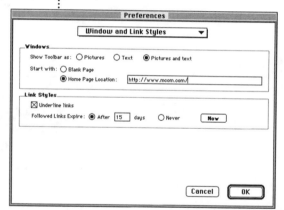

Figure 3-27: *The Window and Link Styles
dialog box in Preferences has to do with the
look of your Netscape screen and your home
page location.*

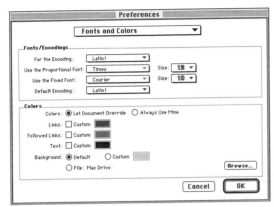

Figure 3-28: *You can customize the colors Netscape uses and choose font displays here.*

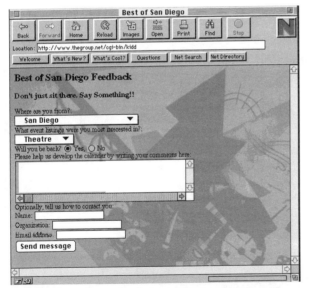

Figure 3-29: *A Kandinsky painting in .GIF form shows an ambitious use of the background option in the Fonts and Colors Preferences box.*

propriate word(s). Once you have visited a page, its link changes color from blue to red by default—a nice feature that shows you at a glance which of the links you have already followed. You can change these colors in the next Preference box: Fonts and Colors.

To say that the Web changes frequently is the understatement of the year—so it makes little sense for your followed links to be in a different color forever. The remaining buttons on the Styles box let you say when you want links to expire (meaning revert to the same display as links you have never followed). One option is Now, another is Never, and you can specify any number of days in between.

Fonts & Colors

If you're the kind of person who loves to play with your screen colors and fonts to suit your mood—blue for Monday, orange for Halloween, green on the first day of spring, etc.—you're going to love this box. Here's where you can play designer to your heart's content. You can choose the colors to display link text in and define a background color for your Netscape screen. If you want to get really creative, try choosing any .GIF you have on hand as a background. Simply select the File button under Background and choose the .GIF by browsing your folders and files. Netscape will present the .GIF (tiled to fill the screen if it's small) as a "desktop" background for your screen. See Figure 3-29 for an example (see "Manipulating Kandinsky" on page 62 for how we created the image). Pop-up menus allow you to select from the fonts on hand for the general text on your page.

Netscape has built-in support for browsing the Web in Japanese and accessing Japanese Web sites. The Encoding box includes settings for three major Japanese character set encodings. To browse the Web in Japanese on the Macintosh, you will need either KanjiTalk 7 or Japanese Language Kit (on System 7). More information on browsing the Web in Japanese will be available on Netscape's home page.

Mail & News

In order to use Netscape's outgoing mail feature to send e-mail, you will need to tell it the details of your mail server. Filling in your name and e-mail address is also well worthwhile—for the keystrokes it will save when it's time to mail something. If you have a signature file you usually attach to outgoing mail, you can tell Netscape where to find it.

The News box has to do with Netscape's USENET News service, and you have to pay some attention to this or you won't be getting any news. First, you must fill in the Internet address of your news server. This is the computer that your system uses to gather USENET news files. All newsreaders need to be told this, and if you don't know it, ask your sysadmin or service provider. It's possible that your News server and your Mail server are the same machine, but not very likely.

Cache & Network

Here's where you can specify how much memory and disk space you want to make available for the cache, according to the size of your system. If you do a lot of heavy-duty Web browsing, the disk cache can fill up very quickly, and it does not clear when you end your Netscape session. You can clear it with the Clear Disk Cache Now button. You might also use this when you have reason to suspect that a page is loading from cache rather than the online

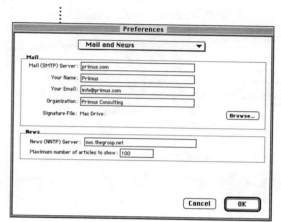

Figure 3-30: *In this box you need to tell Netscape about your mail server and news server.*

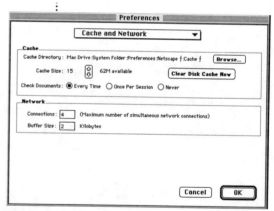

Figure 3-31: *Here's where you manage your cache and network buffer.*

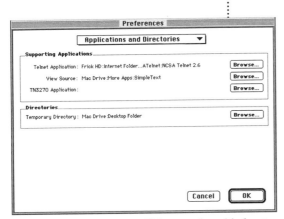

Figure 3-32: *Netscape will have to be told about any TELNET application you use here. You can also change the temporary directory.*

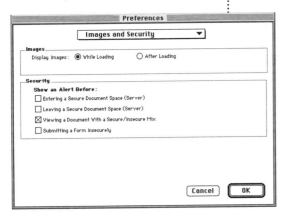

Figure 3-33: *You can choose how you want to view images and whether you want to receive security alerts in this box.*

source, and therefore showing you a version that's out of date.

The Network box allows you to specify the number of simultaneous connections you'd like—that is, how many different Netscape windows you want to run at one time—and the size of the buffer for downloading them (for more windows you'll need more buffer space).

Applications & Directories

The Supporting Applications box is where you enter the location and name of helper applications for TELNET sessions (see Chapter 4) or any application you'd like to use to display (and possibly also edit, save, etc.) source code files—SimpleText would be the most likely default.

The Directories box allows you to change the default location of the temporary files. Temporary files are created by Netscape whenever it is about to use a helper application to display something. After shuttling the helper application and its data file in and out of memory, the temporary file is automatically deleted.

Images & Security

Netscape will normally show you the images in a Web page line by line as they come down. If the images are particularly large, this can take a long time. If you'd prefer not to have the images displayed until the entire file has been downloaded, you can check the After Loading radio button in the Images box in this window.

In the Security box you can specify whether you want to be advised when entering or leaving a secure page or submitting information on an insecure page. Security features are only available on specifically designed Web pages. In general you should assume information you submit on forms is insecure unless otherwise advised.

Proxies

If your Internet connection is through a large company or institution, it's possible that you're working behind what's called a fire wall. This is a device used to ensure the security of their system from outside hackers. If this is the case, you'll need to make use of something called a "proxy" to make your Internet connection. You needn't concern yourself with the technicalities of all this, and neither will we, since it's too variable. Just ask your systems administrator what you need to put in this box to make your connections for the different Internet functions you use.

Helper Applications

Netscape has its own built-in viewer that displays images in .GIF, .JPEG and .XBM format. However, the viewer is not as versatile as a dedicated image-viewer like JPEGView. And Netscape has (so far) no built-in application to run movies, hear audio, or deal with many, many file types you may find yourself bringing to your computer with Netscape's help.

This screen displays and manages a list of all these file types. Netscape should already have taken account of the applications you have on board and you will see them displayed in the Application column. If you have no application for a particular file type, it will appear as Unknown. Don't worry—you can add them later. We'll be talking about these in more detail in Chapter 4.

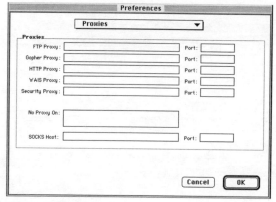

Figure 3-34: *If you're working behind a "fire wall" (frequently used in large businesses) you'll need to fill in this box to make your Internet connections.*

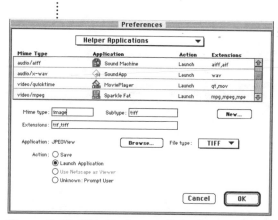

Figure 3-35: *This Preference dialog box confirms that Netscape will use the helper applications Sound Machine and SoundApp for audio and MoviePlayer and Sparkle for video files.*

Customizing Netscape for Multiple Users

With all the options available to you to customize Netscape, it's perfectly possible that multiple users on one computer will differ as to how to
set it up. Tim's favorite screen colors are red, white and blue; Jessica
thinks that's garish and prefers tasteful pastels. His bookmarks are
mostly business and technically-oriented; hers are educational sites she
uses in her teaching job. Neither wants to sort through the other's
bookmarks to find their own, and changing the location of the BOOK-
MARKS file in the Preferences/Applications and Directories box every
time is a drag. And whose e-mail address gets precedence in the Mail
and News box? The solution is simple: his and hers NETSCAPE.INI
files.

If separate bookmarks are all you're interested in, the easiest way to
set up a personal copy is to go to your Bookmark editing screen and
use the Export command to export the current bookmarks into a different file. Instead of the default BOOKMARKS, call it "Tim's Netscape,"
for instance. This will give Tim a separate icon to click on to start
Netscape with his own bookmark list.

If you want full customization—including your own e-mail address
and screen choices, for instance—create a separate copy of the Netscape
Preferences ƒ folder in the System folder. Then launch Netscape by
clicking on the Netscape Preferences file and customize it to your
heart's content.

Moving On

If you're like most people, you will continue to discover new features of Netscape as you use it. By now, besides learning how to navigate around the Web with Netscape you should have learned how to do the following:

- Change the look of your screen to suit you, including gaining maximum screen space when you want it.
- Handle files you want to save, send to someone or manipulate.
- Set up your bookmark list and manage it as it grows.
- Set up Netscape to handle mail and newsreading functions and customize it for your own system and preferences.

In the next chapter we'll go into some of the special features you'll want to use, including using Netscape to do FTP, search the Net and access newsgroups. We'll also look at some of the types of pages you can find on the Web to give you some starting points for exploration.

Manipulating Kandinsky   The background of Figure 3-29 is a painting by Vasily Kandinsky called "On White II." Here's how we did it:

We grabbed the picture from the WebMuseum Paris as a full-color JPEG (see "How We Raided the Louvre" in Chapter 5). Then, using a combination of LVIEW and Collage Image Manager, we took the liberty of rotating it 90 degrees, converting it to a 16-level grayscale .GIF, reducing its contrast and finally boosting the gamma correction to 80. Then we just entered its path and filename in the box provided. You can do the same with whatever you'd like to see behind your Web pages: Your dream rose-covered cottage, the sled you owned as a boy, or a picture of your spouse. Whatever....

Using a largish background like this causes Netscape to pause for file-loading—but only for the first screen of your session. Thereafter, the background artwork loads instantly from cache.

LAUNCHING INTO CYBERSPACE

Being inveterate travelers, the first thing we do when we arrive in a strange city is take off on a walking tour. We're usually too anxious to have a look around to bother with a map, and we've had plenty of time to peruse the travel guides at home.

You've probably felt the same about this new cybercommunity you've just discovered. Unless you're an extremely methodical person, you probably didn't wait to get all your helper applications installed before you took off on your first walk around the Web neighborhood.

So in this chapter we'll take a closer look at things like movie and audio files and in-line images and the helper applications you need to run them. You'll find out how to download hypermedia files and save them for off-line replay, and how to copy images you might want to use in your own documents. We'll show you the kinds of Web pages that are available online, to give you a starting point for your own explorations.

Then we'll talk about those all-important Internet features like FTP, TELNET, Gopher and USENET that are all made available to you in a new easy format with Netscape's interface. And finally we'll tell you how to keep abreast of program updates and point you to some information sites and newsgroups that will help you sort out any problems you have.

Hypermedia in Netscape

If you're to get the best out of the Web experience, you need to understand how hypermedia is presented to you—that way you'll appreciate better what is and isn't possible.

A good example is the difference between an "in-line" image and an "external" image. It's much *less* important to understand the difference between .GIF, .JPEG, and the other half dozen or so image formats—so let's get that out of the way quickly.

Still Photos: .GIFs & .JPEGs

Those alphabet soup file extensions all refer to different ways of encoding a picture for storage as an ordinary computer data file. The granddaddy of them all is .TIFF—the Tagged Image File Format, which creates humongous files. Many other formats, including the very popular .GIF (Graphics Interchange Format), were invented in an attempt to compress the data more effectively. A few years ago, an expert committee called the Joint Photographic Experts Group thrashed out a new format which was supposed to supplant all others and become an industry standard. Hence the .JPEG (or .JPG) format, which has so far failed to become the standard—but it may nevertheless be the best.

Still Photos: In-Lines & Externals

For a not-very-complex color picture, it's generally true to say .GIF is the most compact format but .JPEG offers better quality in the end.

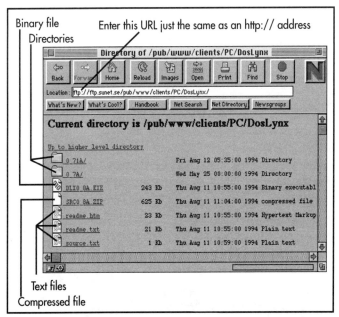

Figure 4-1: *The small in-line image of Dali's Visage of War is .GIF, but the actual image we'll download is a .JPEG, with much finer detail.*

Hence, .GIF is the format invariably used to create all the little "thumbnail" images that decorate Web pages. Data compression, in this case, is more important than quality. Because they are really considered part of the document (even though you can choose not to see them by unchecking Auto Load Images in the Options pull-down menu) they're known as in-line images. In our own Web page design we are careful not to be carried away using these, simply because they can slow down page-loading so much.

An external image is not part of the document you load, but it is referenced by a *link*—either hypertext, like an underlined word, or another type of link. It's these external images that are frequently in .JPEG format, because load time can (within reason!) be sacrificed for quality. Where it gets confusing is when an in-line .GIF is used as the link to an external .JPEG. It's actually a very common technique—used in the Dali exhibit of the "WebMuseum" depicted in Figure 4-1. Perhaps now you can better understand why this is often done.

When you download an external image in .GIF, .JPEG or .XBM format, you can use Netscape's own built-in viewer to see it right there in the content window (here's where you may want to enlarge your window by unchecking the Show Toolbar, Location and Directory Buttons in the Options pull-down menu). For any other image format, you will need a "helper application" in the form of a viewer.

Actually, we recommend that you get and install the helper called JPEGView, and use it for images you especially prize even if they're in .GIF format. For one thing, JPEGView lets you manipulate the image in ways Netscape's own viewer doesn't even attempt. For another, in dealing with external images you have only the View or Save option. There is no option to View *then* Save. This means that you may have spent a little time finding that Dali picture and then only view it fleetingly rather than adding it to a collection.

Set your application to Save in the Preferences/Helper Applications dialog box (see Figure 3-35 and accompanying text in Chapter 3). JPEGView is available at

ftp://ftp.ncsa.uiuc.edu/Mac/Mosaic/Helpers

The file is **jpeg-view-331.hqx**

From now on we will give FTP addresses in the form of URLs as above. You'll find that using Netscape to retrieve documents by FTP will be very handy, especially since it makes cruising directories so easy. See the section on FTP later in this chapter for more explanation.

QuickTime & MPEG Movies

Fortunately, on-Web movies do not come in such a bewildering variety of formats and flavors. Most of them, perhaps 99 percent, are either in the Macintosh standard known as QuickTime, or are the product of another expert committee, the Motion Picture Experts Group—guess what? An .MPEG, of course.

Netscape has no built-in movie viewer, and you really need helpers for both .MPEG and QuickTime formats, since they are about equally common. The eventual image quality is about the same, but QuickTime is a better bet if you want to try for sound in sync. Until this technology moves on a bit, don't expect movie-theater quality. We recommend that you set your helper application preference to Save rather than Launch Application because downloading a movie file

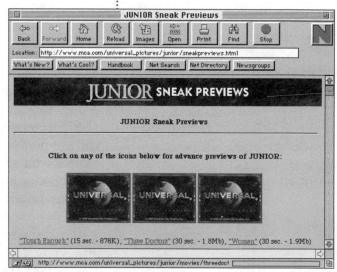

Figure 4-2: *Take advantage of Universal's new sneak previews with a movie player application.*

takes a while, and if there's a last-minute accident at least you won't have to go through that again. (See Figure 3-35 in Chapter 3.)

If you're equipped with movie helpers, you can enjoy Web services like Universal's new sneak previews (Figure 4-2). The best movie player is Sparkle, a freeware program you can get at

ftp://ftp.ncsa.uiuc.edu/Mosaic/Mac/Helpers

The file is **sparkle-231.hqx** (about 2 mb disk space needed)

Sparkle uses the QuickTime movie controller to play MPEGs and it saves MPEGs to QuickTime movies. For that reason, you'll also need the QuickTime software. You'll also need Thread Manager (which is built into System 7.5) from Apple's FTP site at

ftp://ftp.apple.com/Apple.support.Area/Apple.Software.Updates/ US/Macintosh/system.software/Other.System.Software

QuickTime 2.0 is available for $9.95 at **http://quicktime.apple.com**, or **e-mail: quicktime @applelink.apple.com.** You'll be given ordering instructions by credit card through a combination of e-mail and telephone to keep the transaction secure.

You can experiment with a number of other QuickTime players available at the Mac archive sites. They include BijouPlay and PetersPlayer (both of these are simple QT players for 68K and PowerMacs), FastPlayer and EasyPlay. Peruse the Mac archives at

ftp://mac.archive.umich.edu/mac/

This very busy site will send you to one of its mirror sites automatically if you enter **ftp://mirror.archive.umich.edu**

You'll find the viewers in the **/graphics/quicktime** subdirectory.

Audio

The surprising thing about Web audio files, at least to those of us who are nonexperts, is that they are as huge as—and sometimes even huger than—video files. It's not uncommon to find a sound bite lasting just 30 seconds taking up several megabytes of disk space.

A really well-behaved Web page (like the ones we design, natch) tells you how big an audio or video file is, so you can decide whether you have that much time to spend downloading it. Unfortunately, many HTML authors get too carried away by their artistic page makeup to worry about "technical details" like that (or are working on university supercomputers and don't think about those of us on our little home machines), and the information is not available. Netscape helps things along, actually—it will generally give you progress information at the lower left corner of the screen. So if you're already running late for an appointment and you see "12% of 456K read" down there, that's when you click on Stop to bail out.

The icon shown in Figure 4-3 is actually from a "First Family" page from The White House (**http://www.whitehouse.gov**), and it's nice of them to tell us that the sound of Socks mewing is a 36k file. They might have added that it's in .AU format to be *really* helpful.

Our advice is the same as for movie files: Set your helper applications to save rather than launch your application immediately. We'll add more advice, too: Don't let these things accumulate on your disk— they're just too big to give house-room to unless you have good reason.

A good Mac audio player is Sound Machine, which you can find at **ftp://ftp.ncsa.uiuc.edu/Mac/Mosaic/Helpers**
The file is **sound-machine-21.hqx**
There are several other sound utilities you can find at Mac archive sites.

(~36K)

Figure 4-3: *The little icon you will often see as a link to an audio file.*

Forms

There are many times when it's appropriate for the flow of information from the Web to you to be put in reverse: when you need to put information in rather than pull it out. One simple case in point is searching for keywords—how's a Web crawler to know what *you* want to know if you can't tell it?

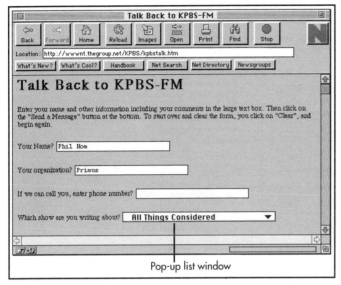

Figure 4-4: *In this local radio feedback page designed by Mark Burgess, "All Things Considered" was selected from a pop-up list of all NPR's regular programs.*

Another good example is a feedback page, on which somebody invites you to enter some information. Netscape invites your feedback in a page you'll find under "How to Give Feedback" in the main menu's Help pull-down. Another example is shown in Figure 4-4. All such page features are known collectively as "forms," and they seem to get more complex and more ingenious all the time.

Undoubtedly, one of the driving forces behind the development of forms is Web commerce. Figure 4-5 shows an order form (for fresh flowers, in this case) complete with credit card information.

Exploring Cyberspace

The day when dry tomes from the catacombs of science and esoteric discussions of quarks dominated the Web is fast disappearing. There are still tons of good references for real and would-be scientists on the Web—in fact, they form a strong backbone to the system. But the number of sites devoted to the wide range of human interests is expanding daily on the Web.

Among the types of Web sites you can visit now are electronic newspapers and magazines, museums and art galleries, entertainment resources, business and commercial outlets, along with many sites run by government, academic or private institutions sharing their own special databases and information.

To give you a feel for the diversity of the Web, we've collected some outstanding sites in various categories. We've even made it easy for you by including them in our Netscape Quick Tour Online Companion. Go to **http://www. vmedia.com/** and you'll find hypertext links to all of the sites listed below and in Chapter 6, as well as links to other Web resources. Take them as starting points and then wander at will. To quote Dr. Seuss, "Oh, the places you'll go!"

Electronic Publications

Time-Life Publishing

Here you can find an online edition of *Time* magazine with excerpts from the latest issue, as well as excerpts from several other magazines owned by Time-Life, such as *Southern Living, Sunset* and *Entertainment Weekly*. You can choose a low-speed (fewer graphics) or high-speed (more goodies) version to suit your taste and computer capacity. *Entertainment Weekly*'s capsule movie reviews are a particularly nice resource.

http://www.timeinc.com/pathfinder/

Hotwired

"Hotwired" is the online version of *Wired* magazine, where all the techno-hip cognoscenti hang out. The graphics on its online edition are really exceptional, and the publication is state-of-the-art in Web publishing.

http://www.wired.com

Some other magazines to peruse:

Boardwatch: **http://www.boardwatch.com**

Mother Jones: **http://www.mojones.com/motherjones.html**

VIBE: **http://www.timeinc.com/vibe/VibeOnline!.html**

Washington Weekly: **http://dolphin.gulf.net**

PC Week and *PC Magazine:* **http://www.ziff.com**

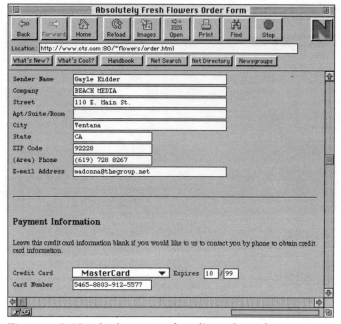

Figure 4-5: *No, that's not a real credit card number—are you kidding?*

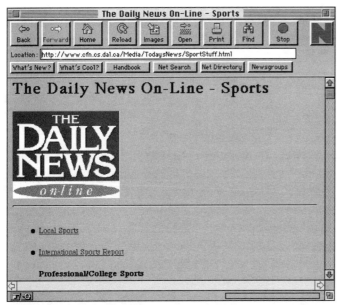

The Daily News On-Line - Sports

Location: http://www.cfn.cs.dal.ca/Media/TodaysNews/SportStuff.html

What's New? What's Cool? Handbook Net Search Net Directory Newsgroups

The Daily News On-Line - Sports

THE
DAILY
NEWS
online

- Local Sports

- International Sports Report

Professional/College Sports

Figure 4-6: *This Canadian page is a great starting point for sports fans.*

News & Sports

A whole host of newspapers are jumping into the online publishing arena. One of the best lists of online newspapers is maintained at **http://www.nando.net/epage/htdocs/links/newspapers.html**.

Among the news sources with links to this page are *USA Today*, the *San Francisco Chronicle & Examiner*, *San Jose Mercury News*, *St. Petersburg Press*, *Boston Globe*, CNN Headline News, Canadian Broadcasting Corporation News, and the *Times* literary supplement (London). For international news links, go to **http://www.cs.vu.nl/~gerben/news.html**.

Sports news and the latest scores in football, basketball, baseball, hockey and soccer are a popular resource at **http://www.cfn.cs.dal.ca/Media/TodaysNews/SportStuff.html**

More football scores at **http://www.nando.net/football/1994/fbserv.html**

The latest tennis rankings and results can be found at **http://arganet.tenagra.com/Racquet_Workshop/Workshop.html**

Create Your Own Newspaper

You can make up your own newspaper from the available Web offerings and save it with links for future use at this clever Web site: **http://sun.bucknell.edu/~boulter/crayon/**

Museums & Art Galleries

The Web Museum, Paris (Le WebLouvre)

Nicolas Pioch, who maintains this page, had to stop calling it "Le WebLouvre" after an icy letter from lawyers representing the Ministry of Cultural Affairs. *Lese majesté* notwithstanding, this is the model that many other museums are trying to follow as they go online. See highlights of exhibits at the Louvre in Paris and as an added attraction, take a "walking tour" of Paris. Nobody knows a good tourist lure like the Parisians.

http://mistral.enst.fr/louvre/

There are many mirror sites all over the world, and the idea is to relieve the immense load on the original computer in Paris. On the east coast of the US, there's **http://sunsite.unc.edu/louvre**, and we Californians should (and do) use **http://www.emf.net/louvre** at Berkeley.

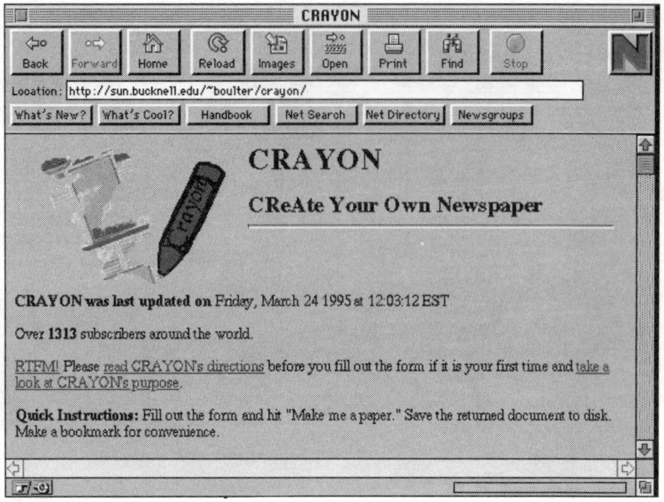

Figure 4-7: *Make up your own newspaper from available Web offerings at this creative site.*

The Smithsonian

Visit the Smithsonian Institution in Washington, D.C., and you'll find a wealth of resources for teachers, students and the aimlessly curious. You can view collections at the National Museum of Natural History and the National Air & Space Museum, or use the Smithsonian Education Server.

http://www.si.edu

The Exploratorium

The online interface of this many-faceted museum in the Palace of Fine Arts in San Francisco is a labyrinth for exploring science and nature topics.

http://www.exploratorium.edu

Scripps Institution of Oceanography

The aquarium-museum at this landmark oceanographic institution on the Pacific shores in San Diego has information on marine animals, tide pools, and current research on the oceans and atmosphere.
http://aqua.ucsd.edu

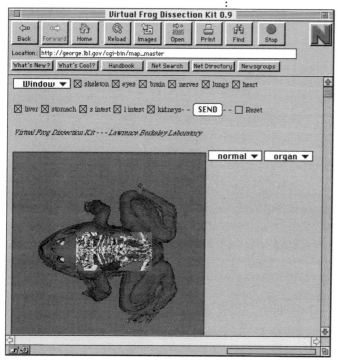

Figure 4-8: *The World Wide Web must have saved the lives of a few thousand frogs already.*

Educational Resources

The Village Schoolhouse

Dozens of resources for teachers, students and home-schoolers. New projects being added constantly. Teachers can visit the K-12 Teacher's Lounge and exchange projects and information.
http://crusher.bev.net:80/education/index.html

Curry School

The Curry School at the University of Virginia is dedicated to encouraging interactive education with computers for kids. This is another rich source of educational materials for elementary and high school teachers and students.
http://curry.edschool.virginia.edu

Sea World/Busch Gardens

Sea World maintains a great animal database, useful for teachers and students alike.
http://crusher.bev.net:80/education/SeaWorld

Virtual Frogs

It had to happen: dissecting cyberfrogs. Two sites have actually come up with their demo projects for school use, one run by Lawrence Berkeley

Laboratories (Figure 4-8), the other by Curry School at the University of Virginia. Try your lab skills at
http://george.lbl.gov/ITG.hm.pg.docs/dissect/info.html
http://curry.edschool.virginia.edu/~insttech/frog

The SILS Clearinghouse

The University of Michigan's School of Information and Library Studies maintains an ongoing reference called the **Clearinghouse for Subject-Oriented Internet Resource Guides**. This is a collection of specially written documents categorized under Humanities, Sciences, Ecology, etc. All of them are lavishly hyperlinked to other net resources, and anybody can create their own document and submit it for inclusion in this wonderful educational Web page.
http://http2.sils.umich.edu/~lou/chhome.html

American Memory Project

The Library of Congress sponsors this Web site in progress, which contains a collection of primary source and archival material on American culture and history. Includes historical photographs from the Civil War to the present, speeches by American leaders during and after World War I and lots of photos and bibliographical material.
http://lcweb2.loc.gov/amhome.html

Government & Institutions

U.S. Government Master Page

This is the central address for government information pages. From here you can split off to your favorite branch—Executive, Legislative or

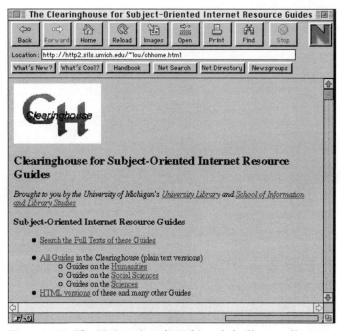

Figure 4-9: *The University of Michigan's brilliant collection of hyperlinked educational resource guides.*

Judicial (remember your civics class?), plus a number of government-related independent agencies like the Small Business Administration. You can even get your tax forms by e-mail.
http://www.alw.nih.gov/govt.html

The White House

If it's the Prez you're interested in, you can skip the previous page and go straight to the White House. Take a tour of the interior or see The Man himself at play with the family cat—who looks like she'd rather be in Arkansas.
http://www.whitehouse.gov

NASA

Seems every Net jockey in the world is interested in rockets and spaceships. NASA's home pages are among the most visited on the Web. Here you can get the latest news on space shuttle missions and view some of the wealth of space imagery generated by NASA's activities, including exploration of the solar system.
http://hypatia.gsfc.nasa.gov/NASA_homepage.html

Business & Commercial

Open Market Inc.

Visit the Open Market for a directory of commercial services, products and information on the Internet. See What's New or search for a product on the Net. Our search for "flowers" turned up 13 online florists.
http://www.directory.net

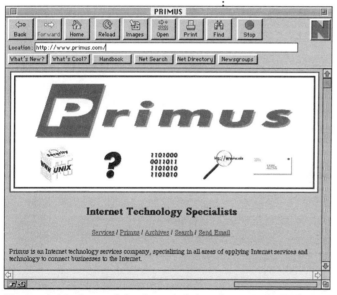

Figure 4-10: *So much business is being done on the Web these days that Web business is a business itself.*

Interesting Business Sites

The businesses in this list are personally selected by Bob O'Keefe at the School of Management, Rensselaer Polytechnic Institute, and updated monthly. He keeps a keen eye out for the latest business developments on the Net.
http://www.rpi.edu/~okeefe/business.html

Internet Business Center

This is a great resource for business activities on the Web—including statistics on the latest commercial sites and traffic.
http://tig.com/IBC/index.html

Stock Market Updates

Several services offer stock quotes and market rates online. For a fee, a number of them allow you to register your portfolio to receive closing prices every day. We like the site run by Security APL Inc., which as a come-on to their services lets you get free quotes, one at a time. Their Market Watch Page is updated every three minutes during trading hours. Access at **http://www.secapl.com**

Databases

U.S. Census Information Server

The Census Bureau posts population statistics, financial data on state and local governments and schools, county and city data—and census bureau publications.
http://www.census.gov/

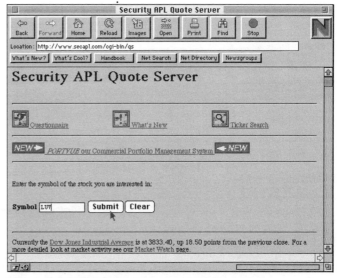

Figure 4-11: *This investment service offers a full range of business information, plus free stock quotes.*

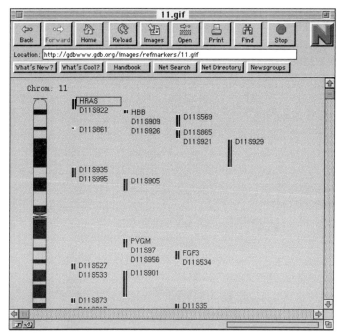

Figure 4-12: *Genetic databases, like this chromosome map, could hardly be bett4r suited to the Internet.*

The Human Genome Project

The Human Genome Project has taken on the monumental task of mapping every chromosome and writing down the complete genetic code that describes a human being, letter by letter. Scientists and medical specialists around the world access this database, which is constantly updated.
http://www.hgmp.mrc.ac.uk/HUMAN-GEN-DB.html

Movies & Entertainment

Cardiff Movie Database Browser

Pages for film buffs and trivia quiz masters. Search for movie titles, actors, directors, what have you.
http://www.cm.cf.ac.uk/Movies/

Movie Studios

Visit the movie studios and see previews of coming attractions in downloadable QuickTime clips. You can even visit the Press Room for coming attractions.
Buena Vista Pictures: **http://bvp.wdp.com:80/index.html**
Universal Pictures: **http://www.mca.com/:80/**

Travel

The London Guide

This is one of our favorite places to visit when one of us (guess which one) gets homesick. Designed by University College, London, these pages are a resource for Londoners and tourists alike, with guides to the theatre scene, pubs, restaurants, hotels and even a "Tube Journey

Planner" which plots your route on the London Underground for you.
http://www.cs.ucl.ac.uk/misc/uk/london.html

The Big Island of Hawaii

Blizzard outside? Think you'll never see the sun again? Take a break and visit Hawaii. Meet the people, tour the countryside and visit the volcanos at this smart site that gives excerpts from the Moon Travel Handbook on Hawaii. This is part of the University of California Irvine's bookstore offerings. Lop off the pathway in the URL address (from the first dash onward) and you can peruse the entire UCI bookstore.
http://bookweb.cwis.uci.edu:8042/Books/Moon/hawaii.html

If daydreaming turns to reality planning, you can actually book a vacation cottage on the beach in Kauai (see Figure 4-13) at
http://www.cerf.net/anini

Personal Home Pages

The World Wide Web Virtual Library Home Page Directory

One of the best resources for interesting Web sites is the hypertext version of word of mouth from other users. If it's cool or interesting, you can bet other people have put it on their private lists, which are often made public at sites like this. This repository of selected home

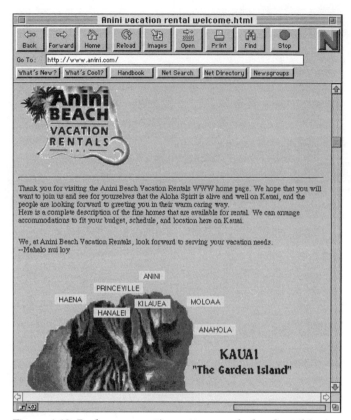

Figure 4-13: *Book your vacation cottage on the beach at this site.*

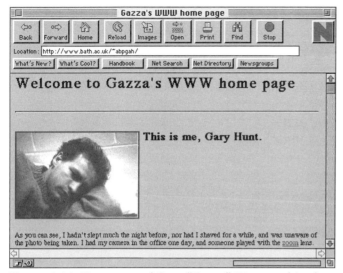

Figure 4-14: *Home page of Gary "Gazza" Hunt—a friend we "met on the Net."*

pages includes those devoted to special interests as well as general resources.

http://web.city.ac.uk/citylive/pages.html

Internet Services via Netscape

After a few weeks of cruising the Web, you get so used to seeing "http://" up there in the URL window that you might start thinking of the entire Internet world in terms of http addresses. In fact, **http** (HyperText Transport Protocol) is the data-exchange protocol that made the Web possible, but it's far from being the only allowable prefix to URL addresses. Actually it merely specifies a type of server—the one whose exact address makes up the next part of the URL.

Almost all the "traditional" Internet protocols have server addresses that are accessible by Netscape. Thus you can construct a URL beginning **gopher://**, **ftp://**, **or telnet://**—and by a kind of trickery, the prefix **mailto:** brings e-mail transmission to your Netscape screen. Even Finger (get login information) and Archie (search FTP sites for keywords) services are available, thanks to so-called "gateways" made available by some major Web servers, and accessed as **http** addresses.

E-Mail

Netscape, as already mentioned, has a fine outgoing mail service accessed from the main menu's File pull-down (Mail Document or ⌘M). It can convey an ordinary e-mail message, or you can include a complete or partial text of the current page or anything on the Clipboard. If you are trying to use this service and getting constant errors, it's likely to be because you have not set your Mail dialog box correctly to point Netscape at your mail server machine. Find the Mail and News dialog box in Preferences on the Options pull-down in the Main menu.

So if you want to send a message to **juliaZ@almond.ulua.edu**, the obvious way is to press ⌘M, enter Julia's address, change the subject header if need be (it defaults to the URL of the current page), make your message and send it. But another way is to turn Julia's address into a pseudo-URL, using the prefix **mailto:**. Select the toolbar Open button and enter **mailto:juliaZ@almond.ulua.edu** in the URL window. You'll find it brings up the e-mail form with the address already filled out and a blank subject header.

So what's the big deal? The big deal is that, since this format is acceptable as a URL address, you can make it into a bookmark like any other. Press ⌘B and bring up the full bookmark edit window. Create a new header called e-mail and then add all your regular correspondents one by one, with their real names in the Name box and their **mailto:** addresses in the Location box. Now when you pull down your bookmark list you'll be able to select "e-mail" then "Julia" using just your keyboard arrow keys or your mouse. Perhaps one of these days you'll even be able to select your message to Julia from a pull-down menu!

FTP

Both of us are old enough Net-jockeys to remember when anonymous FTP (File Transfer Protocol) was a real chore. There was a lot to type— with perfect accuracy—just to get connected. Directory listings would whiz by out of control; you'd have to remember to switch between ASCII and binary modes to get your downloads right; to inspect a

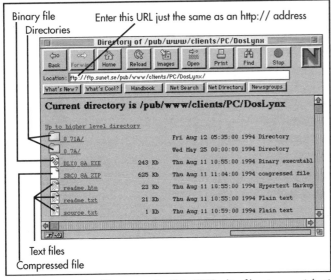

Binary file

Directories

Enter this URL just the same as an http:// address

Directory of /pub/www/clients/PC/DosLynx

| Back | Forward | Home | Reload | Images | Open | Print | Find | Stop |

Location: ftp://ftp.sunet.se/pub/www/clients/PC/DosLynx/

| What's New? | What's Cool? | Handbook | Net Search | Net Directory | Newsgroups |

Current directory is /pub/www/clients/PC/DosLynx

Up to higher level directory

0_71A/		Fri Aug 12 05:35:00 1994 Directory
0_7A/		Wed May 25 00:00:00 1994 Directory
DLX0_8A.EXE	243 Kb	Thu Aug 11 10:55:00 1994 Binary executabl
SRC0_8A.ZIP	625 Kb	Thu Aug 11 11:04:00 1994 compressed file
readme.htm	23 Kb	Thu Aug 11 10:55:00 1994 Hypertext Markup
readme.txt	21 Kb	Thu Aug 11 10:55:00 1994 Plain text
source.txt	1 Kb	Thu Aug 11 10:59:00 1994 Plain text

Text files

Compressed file

Figure 4-15: *The file names in this FTP site directory act just like hypertext links—click 'em and grab 'em.*

README file you'd have to pipe it through a separate UNIX pager; and in general the command set was about what you'd expect for one of the oldest forms of Internetting there is.

The first move in the direction of user-friendliness was the invention of the UNIX program **ncftp**, which at least logged on for you, remembered your favorite sites and directories and provided a way of displaying all those README files. Today, special FTP applications like Fetch easily handle automatic login, scrolling of directory listings, and README by mouse.

Netscape has one of the best FTP programs there is—it does all that, plus displaying directory listings with an icon accompanying each entry showing what type of file it is (see Figure 4-15). When it comes to a download, you don't have to decide whether this is supposed to be binary or ASCII: Netscape knows already. When you click on a file icon, Netscape follows whatever instructions you have given it on how to handle file types (Preferences/Helper Applications). This will normally be "Display a text file—Save a binary to disk."

⟲ HOT TIP

Keep a list of your often-visited FTP sites in a special bookmark subdirectory. Their URL addresses all begin "ftp://...." and often "ftp" appears twice in the complete address—for example **ftp://ftp.digital.com**.

Gopher

The Internet Gopher was always a much friendlier way of accessing what's out there: It actually reads many of the same data sources that FTP and TELNET and WAIS do, but it strips out the jargon and reduces everything to a menu choice. You can start anywhere and get anywhere from any starting point in the great labyrinth of Gopher-burrows. One good starting point is the "Gopher Jewels" menu maintained by the University of Southern California. Its URL is **gopher://cwis.usc.edu:70/ 11/Other_Gophers_and_Information_Resources/Gopher-Jewels**.

One difficulty we always had when searching for something with the Gopher was remembering which Gopher-burrows we had already explored. Netscape's color change for "followed links" applies as much to Gopher menu items as it does to Web pages, and it's a terrific help. So is the Back button.

In a sense, the philosophy of the Gopher, invented at the University of Minnesota, laid the groundwork for the World Wide Web by showing that Internet resources could be made accessible to people who did not care to learn FTP commands and never found out the difference between a binary and an ASCII file transfer. Now the Gopher may be a victim of the phenomenal success of the Web. One Gopher site we've used more times than we could count has just announced that it is going "out of business" in favor of a super-duper Web page.

TELNET

Like Gopher, many of the services offered by TELNET are being revised these days into a more easily accessible Web format. The TELNET protocol is the one you use to connect your computer directly to another computer, which may be in Australia as easily as in Washington DC.

We used to TELNET often to the library of Dartmouth College (**baker.dartmouth.edu**) to use their searchable Shakespeare to help with the cryptic crosswords we're addicted to. Now that we've discovered the hypertext Shakespeare (**http://the-tech.mit.edu/Shakespeare/works.html**), we won't be going to Dartmouth so often. However, TELNET is far from obsolete—if you ever need to do any serious database searching, you're going to get to know TELNET, and the WAIS services (Wide Area Information Services) TELNET can get you to.

Netscape needs helper software to complete a TELNET connection. NCSA Telnet is a good one that you can find in the Mac archives at many FTP sites. You will need to tell Netscape about it in the Applications and Directories box of the Preferences menu.

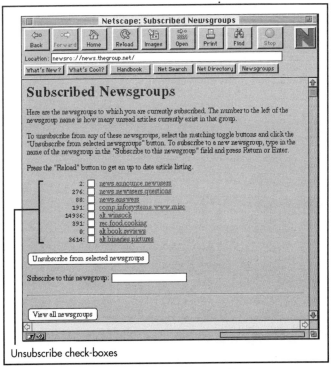

Unsubscribe check-boxes

Figure 4-16: *Netscape's main newsgroup display.*

USENET Newsgroups

You get to Netscape's newsreader from the Directory pull-down menu. However, before using this feature, refer to the note in Chapter 3 on Mail and News in the Preferences menu. You'll need to tell Netscape the name of your NNTP server, and if you're already a case-hardened USENET freak, you may be able to import an existing NEWSRC file (it's the file that keeps track of what newsgroups you're subscribed to and what articles you've already read). If you don't have a pre-existing NEWSRC file, the first time you call up the newsgroups, Netscape will kindly create one for you. It will subscribe you to the three "newbie" newsgroups, **news.announce.newusers**, **news.newusers.questions**, and **news.answers**.

If you do already have a NEWSRC file, simply copy it into the Netscape/Preferences area of the System Folder. All of your regular newsgroups will appear on Netscape's subscription list.

Netscape's built-in newsreader is good. So good that we can't really do justice to all of its features in this book. Notice the numbers to the left of the Unsubscribe checkboxes in Figure 4-16? It's the number of unread articles in that group—you'd be amazed how very few newsreaders provide that information.

Now click on one of the newsgroup names and see the layout of article titles. (See Figure 4-17.) Each article is accompanied by a count of the number of text lines in it. And all that indenting and subtitling is also a "deluxe" feature: this reader is what's known as "threaded," meaning that all articles on the same topic are grouped together.

From the Newsgroup screen you have several options, displayed as clickable items on your screen, including Post Article (brings up the Mail screen filled out to the current newsgroup), as well as Catchup and Show All Articles. Go to reading any article and you've got another set of options (see Figure 4-18), including Catchup Thread, Post Followup and Reply to Sender—the last two bring up the Mail screen again, and you can include the text of the current article with the Quote Document button (see Figure 4-19). All the options are displayed at both the top and bottom of the Newsgroup screens, so you needn't scroll back to the beginning when you've finished reading.

To subscribe to a new newsgroup, it helps to know its full name so that you can simply write it in. To browse all newsgroups, you'll have to select the View All Newsgroups button in the main Newsgroup page, and downloading all those names takes a while. To unsubscribe

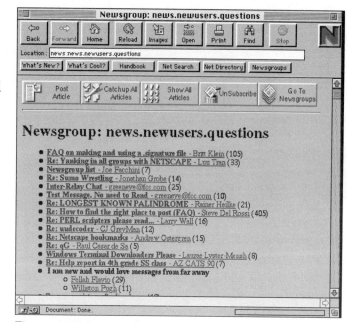

Figure 4-17: *Layout of the article list makes it easy to see the threads.*

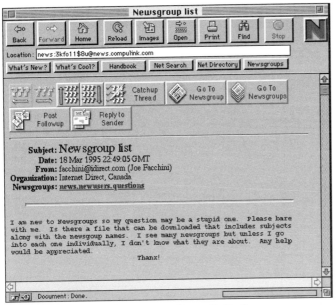

Figure 4-18: *All options are easily available from your newsreading screen.*

to a group, you have two choices: (1) click on the check box beside that group in your main subscription list then select the Unsubscribe From Selected Newsgroups button, or (2) use the Unsubscribe button at the top or the bottom of the list of articles in the group.

Note: Some earlier versions of Netscape lacked the View All Newsgroups button. If you're working with one of these, see Appendix A for an alternative.

Another fab feature that Netscape claims as unique (and we would not dispute the claim) is its ability to find and interpret hypertext links and HTML formatting in news articles. To see this, subscribe to one of the newsgroups that discusses the Web, like **comp.infosystems.www.misc** (you'll find Netscape announcements and bug discussions here). Many of the articles will be "signed" with a hypertext link to the author's home page, or they may contain links to images, other URLs, whatever HTML can provide. If you want to include HTML codes in a posting of your own, enclose a section of your article within the coding <HTML>.....</HTML>. But bear in mind that only Netscape users will see it as you intend.

Archie

Archie is the Internet service that allows you to search every FTP site in the world for directory and file names containing a keyword that you're interested in—"beatle," let's say. Even though there's no such thing as a URL beginning "archie://..." this wonderful service is available on the Web thanks to a so-called hypertext "gateway" provided by NCSA.

Go to **http://hoohoo.ncsa.uiuc.edu/archie.html** to find all the Archie commands all wrapped up in one fill-out-and-submit Web page (see Figures 4-20 and 4-21).

First is a box for you to enter your keyword(s). Then comes a pop-up menu of four different search types. The default is not case-sensitive and searches for the string, not the word (which means that "Beatles" would be found by searching for "beatle"). Radio buttons allow you to pick between a sort by Host computer or by Date. Another pop-up allows you to choose the "niceness" rating of your search— Nicest/Extremely Nice/Very Nice/Nicer/Nice/Not Nice At All. Archie servers are in demand, and there's always a queue of users waiting for search results. Niceness is basically a way of saying "After you—I insist" or "Do you mind?—I'm in a real hurry." If you accept the default Very Nice, you will barge ahead of somebody who has rated her search Nicest. (We're looking forward to the day when this menu comes up changed to Polite/Cool/Supercilious/Bloody Rude.) If you're not in a hurry and can do something else meanwhile, you might consider being Extremely Nice.

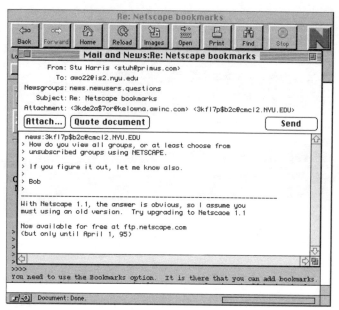

Figure 4-19: *A news follow-up window. Netscape practically writes it for you.*

One more pop-up list is a selection of Archie servers. Pick one that's geographically close (Internic, in California just a few miles from us, is one of our favorites). Finally, you have options to restrict the search by domain and number of hits. All this to save you from having to compose a UNIX command like

archie -s -m100 -N5000 beatle.

Searches can take a while—the nicer, the longer, obviously—but Netscape makes life very easy once the results are in. The hit list becomes a hypertext document which you can scroll, save or click on to go

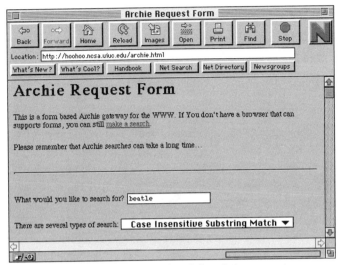

Figure 4-20: *This search for "beatle" took just over two minutes and produced 33 files to choose from.*

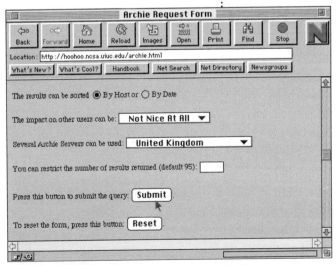

Figure 4-21: *Some of the options on the Archie request form at NCSA.*

straight to the likeliest source of that Beatles lyric you were looking for. Truly luxurious search-and-grab.

Finger

The Department of Computer Science of the University of Indiana has kindly provided another hypertext "gateway"—this one to Finger services. Its address is **http://www.cs.indiana.edu/finger/**.

Finger was originally used in UNIX networks to find out who else is logged on, see when they last checked their e-mail, and consult project files created for that specific purpose. "Project files" has come to mean all sorts of weird things. Add "**dmc.iris.washington.edu/ spyder**" onto the address above, and you'll get a readout of recent seismic events worldwide. California residents can get information about their Congressional representatives by fingering **sen.ca.gov/** followed by their ZIP Code. And then there's always the state of the Coca Cola machine at various US universities. Carnegie-Mellon (**coke.elab.cs.cmu.edu**) was the first to make their coke machine Fingerable, and others have followed. Cyndi Williams provides weekly trivia by Finger at **magnus1.com/cyndiw**. There may also be baseball scores, weather forecasts, and Nielsen ratings out there in Finger-space—the sites change too frequently for a book to be a very reliable source of good Finger addresses.

In general, a user@host address needs to be formatted as host/user for the Indiana gateway. So to find out about someone whose e-mail address is **ualee@mcl.ucsb.edu**, you have to type: **http://www.cs.indiana.edu/finger/mcl.ucsb.edu/ualee**.

If you don't specify a user, you are likely to get a readout of everyone logged in to that host machine (see Figure 4-22).

The actual source of the information Finger conveys is the first line of a file called ".project," and the whole of a file called ".plan" (these conventions originated at UC Berkeley). One or both have to be present in the user's home directory. So if you want to provide some information of interest to somebody who Fingers you, you need to have a UNIX shell account and simply make up those files.

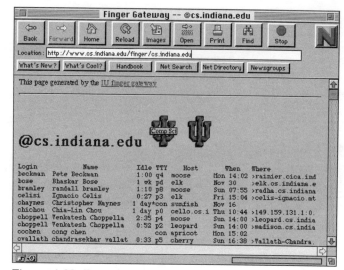

Figure 4-22: *Enter **http://www.cs.indiana.edu/finger/cs.indiana.edu** to find out who's logged on at Indiana right now.*

Staying Current

Just when you think you know everything and are all up to speed, it's bound to happen. New connection services, software updates, new protocols and standards—they'll all come pouring at you, and before you know it you're behind the times again.

Just by checking in to the Web and using its resources regularly you'll undoubtedly stay apprised of the most significant developments.

But here are some places where you can check to find out what's new on the Web and what new geewhizzery is just around the corner.

Getting Updates

Announcements about new updates to Netscape are posted on the Netscape Communications Corporation's home page. Access via the Directory menu—Netscape Communications Corporation. You can also find out about updates to Netscape, as well as to your TCP/IP stack and helper applications, by staying abreast of the USENET newsgroups on Web browsers and reading the recent FAQs.

FAQs & Other Reading Material

Besides Netscape's own online FAQ (accessed via Frequently Asked Questions in the Help pull-down), there are several good FAQs for newsgroups concerned with the Web and Web browsers. They can all be found in Web-browser format in the USENET FAQ archive at Ohio State:

http://www.cis.ohio-state.edu/hypertext/faq/usenet/FAQ-List.html

A particularly useful FAQ is the **comp.infosystems.www** FAQ, which you can also find at

http://sunsite.unc.edu/boutell/faq/www_faq.html

Another good introductory guide to the Web is the WWW Primer, found at

http://www.vuw.ac.nz/who/Nathan.Torkington/ideas/www-primer.html

Information Sites

The WWW Information Site is a good place to start for Web-related information. It has links to several different topics for users, service providers and Web authors. You can find it at

http://www.bsdi.com/server/doc/web-info.html

Scott Yanoff's famous "Special Internet Connections," always a reliable and up-to-date guide to what's good, is now available as a hypertext document at

http://www.uwm.edu/Mirror/inet.services.html

Newsgroups

Several newsgroups are dedicated to exchanging information about Web browsers. They're a good place to ask questions or look for solutions to problems you may have, and also to stay abreast of the latest updates. Some that we've found particularly useful are:

comp.infosystems.www.misc
comp.infosystems.www.providers
comp.infosystems.www.users
comp.infosystems.announce
alt.internet.services

Netscape Corporation's designers often check into these newsgroups to monitor and volunteer information.

Moving On

By now you should be aware that the Web is all things to all people. Perhaps you're still just enjoying exploring, or maybe you've found your own little niche of favorite sites run by like-minded Webbers. Maybe you're feeling like you'd like to stake your claim on a little patch in this frontier.

In the next chapter we'll tell you how to do that. We'll tell you a bit about Web page design and start you off on designing a simple page in HTML. Your imagination and ambition can take off from there.

MAKING YOUR OWN WEB DOCUMENTS

In Chapter 3 you saw how Netscape actually creates a personal Web page for you with the Bookmark menu. It only takes a little imagination to wonder whether you couldn't personalize it a little—say, insert your own picture and some info you'd like to include about yourself—and save it as a home page file.

We'll show you how. And so that you understand all the basics of HTML composition, we'll start fresh and design a complete Web page with in-line images and hypertext links. You'll be able to copy any of our techniques for yourself—and we'll give you detailed instructions on how to exploit the New Age of Plagiarism.

HTML: The Language of the Web

Go to a Web page—any old page will do—and pick the menu choice View/Source. What you see is HTML. Look scary? Awww, c'mon—it's not like a real computer language. At least you can see some ordinary English text in there (okay, if you picked a Spanish site you can see Spanish).

Mixed in with the text, sometimes quite densely, are a lot of things like <H1>, </H1>, <P>, </P>, <A HREF="file">, and so on. Those are just the tags that the Web browser needs to interpret the author's page. In general, they come in pairs such as <H1> for a start tag, </H1> for an end tag. Some HTML authors use lowercase letters—some use a mixture of uppercase and lowercase. Frankly, my dear, the Web doesn't give a damn.

An entire HTML document is (usually) enclosed within a tag pair, like this:

<HTML>
....everything in the document
</HTML>

It needs to be subdivided once only, like this:

<HTML>
<HEAD>
....everything in the header: Title, document type, etc.
</HEAD>
<BODY>
....everything in the body: In other words, everything that's actually going to appear on the page.
</BODY>
</HTML>

Starting with that simple framework, which you can see in Figure 5-1, we're going to build a home page for you visually, explaining each new element as we add it.

Building a Home Page

The way we normally work is to have our HTML text file in SimpleText (or any text editor) in the left two-thirds of the screen, and Netscape up (but not connected to the Net) in the right two-thirds of the screen. They overlap but can be brought into the foreground just by clicking. The local file is loaded into Netscape initially by the menu choice File/Open File, or ⌘O. We use the Reload toolbar button thereafter. After each change we make to the HTML file, we Save the file and Reload the page into Netscape to see what effect our change has had. Since this is a Web document, we usually use the file extension .html (.htm is just as good). File names should be in lowercase if you intend to post them on the Web, since some servers are case-sensitive. Netscape itself does not check files at the door and turn away any that aren't named correctly.

All of the text we want to put in our Web page is defined first as paragraphs. Every paragraph begins with <P> and ends with </P>. HTML ignores all line breaks and carriage returns in a source file, and creates a line break only when it sees </P>. In Figure 5-2, you can see how all of the basic text in our page is set up in eight paragraphs.

Next we'd like to make a proper list out of our travel diary entries. We'll choose the <OL> tag, for an Ordered List. We could have picked <DL>Definition List, <UL>Unordered list, <MENU> or others. We replace the <P> at the beginning of our list text with <OL> and the </P> at the end with </OL>. Then we encase each element in the list within the <LI>...</LI> codes (for List Item). We don't need to add the numbers—Netscape will do that. The results are shown in Figure 5-3.

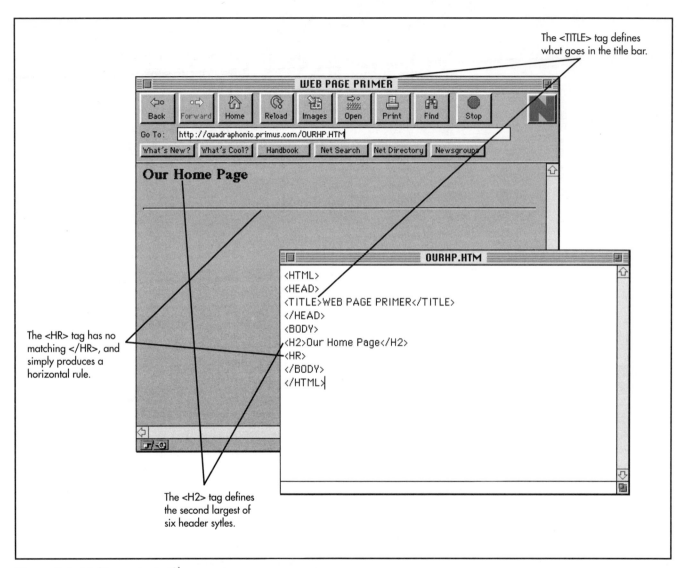

The <TITLE> tag defines what goes in the title bar.

The <HR> tag has no matching </HR>, and simply produces a horizontal rule.

The <H2> tag defines the second largest of six header sytles.

Figure 5-1: *Making a start : three new tags.*

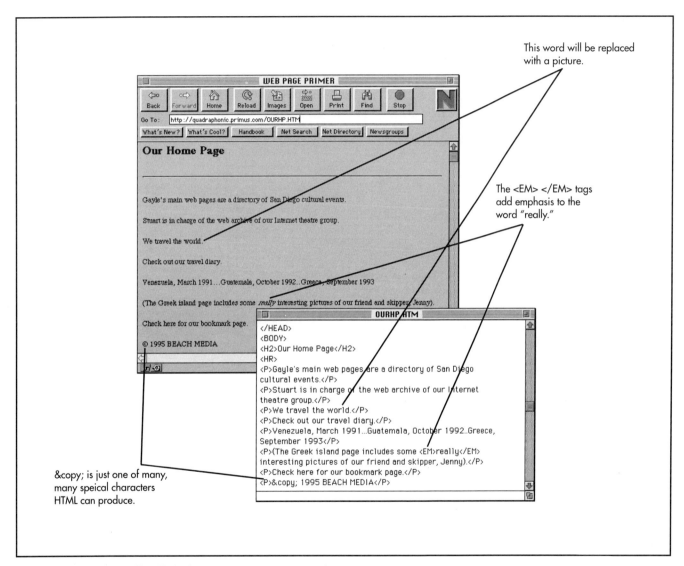

This word will be replaced with a picture.

The <EM> </EM> tags add emphasis to the word "really."

© is just one of many, many speical characters HTML can produce.

Figure 5-2: *This is really all the basic text we want to put in.*

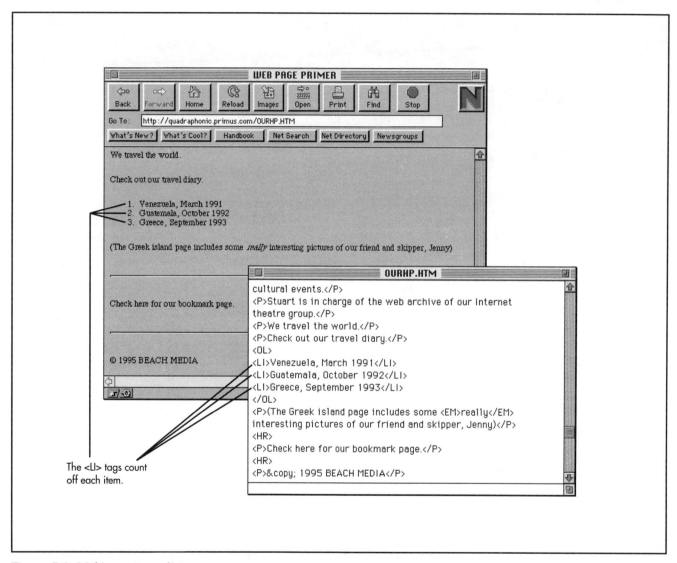

The <LI> tags count
off each item.

Figure 5-3: *Making a proper list.*

Adding Images & Links

As we mentioned before (Chapter 4), in-line "thumbnail" images must be in the .GIF format (actually .XBM and .XPM are allowed, but everybody uses .GIF). If you don't have your own scanner to scan in your favorite holiday snapshots, you'll need to find either a friend with a scanner (such people are getting more and more popular) or a lab that can do it. The lab people will try and blind you with science, but your requirement is simple and straightforward: you need a full-screen color .GIF with the best resolution possible given that you do not want to end up with a data file bigger than, say, 75k. (The size of the file will be much reduced after you crop it and size it for an in-line .GIF.) Anything bigger has more definition than anybody will ever see and will simply make the page slow to load. One service we've used charges $9.95 and they shoot in 24 hours—or faster for more money. These days, if you're lucky, you may even find your local copy shop offering a scan-to-disk service for much less.

You're going to need some image management software to allow you to do your own cropping and sizing. JPEGView works fine for this, and Photoshop is almost overkill. You can play all kinds of fancy games keeping icon libraries and in-line folders, but for the sake of simplicity let's assume the complete kit—the HTML file plus all hypermedia files—is all in your Netscape folder.

So, once you've got the .GIFs all cropped, sized and assembled, you call each of them into your page with the tag <IMG SRC = "filename.gif">. You can see the result in Figure 5-4.

That's already nice, but a couple of adjustments to the "World" in-line are in order. First, it would be nice if the middle of the image lined up with the text rather than the bottom. Second, if we intend to post our page on the Web, we have to bear in mind that not everyone is seeing this page in a graphical Web browser, and many who are may be

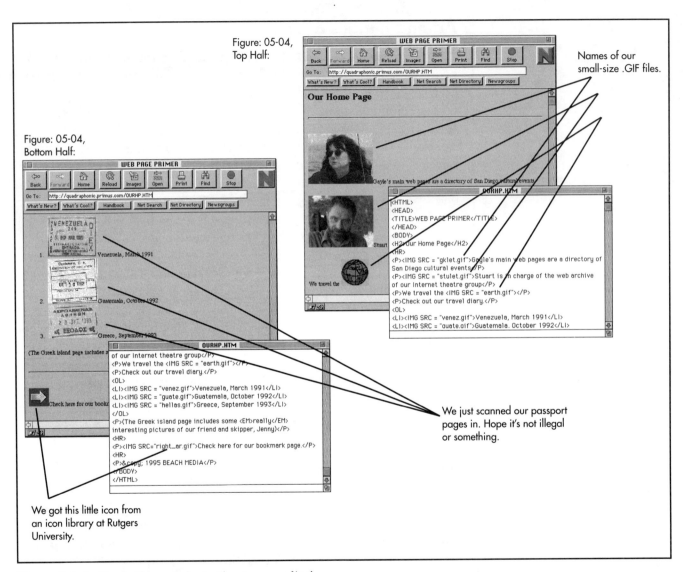

Figure: 05-04,
Top Half:

Names of our
small-size .GIF files.

Figure: 05-04,
Bottom Half:

We just scanned our passport
pages in. Hope it's not illegal
or something.

We got this little icon from
an icon library at Rutgers
University.

Figure 5-4: *Suddenly this page is starting to come alive!*

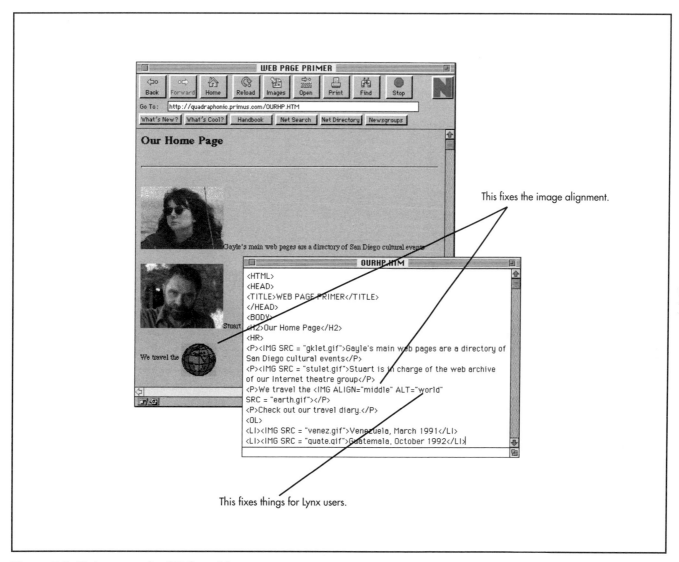

Figure 5-5: *Fixing a couple of little problems.*

speedily surfing the Web with their in-line images turned off. The latest version of Netscape (and some other Web browsers) allows you to see alternate text if you're not using images. But there are also perfectly good—and very fast—text browsers. Lynx is the most popular.

Lynx users, if we don't help them out, will see that line as

"We travel the [IMAGE]"

The way to help them out is to make use of the tag ALT, meaning "If you can't show an image, here's what to replace it with." If you're making your page just for your own use, of course, you needn't bother. Figure 5-5 shows these amendments.

Links

Well, this is supposed to be hypertext, right? It's time we hypered off to some other destinations.

A hypertext link (we'll just call it a link from now on) is signaled by two elements combined. The first is an anchor in the form <A> ...something... </A>, where the something is the word or picture that the user will click on to activate the link. The second is a reference in the form HREF="...something...", and in this case the something is where the link leads to: a different part of this document, another document, an external image or other hypermedia event, or a URL address on a completely different computer, possibly in a different country.

One document we're definitely going to need to link to is our travel diary, which is a separate document in our own computer called "trdiary.htm." To turn the word "Venezuela" into a link to its part of "trdiary.htm" we write the combined tags like this:

<A HREF="trdiary.htm#Lagunetas">Venezuela</A>

That "**#Lagunetas**" tagged onto the file name tells Netscape to go to the internal label "Lagunetas" which is buried somewhere in "trdiary.htm". The matching tag in that file is actually

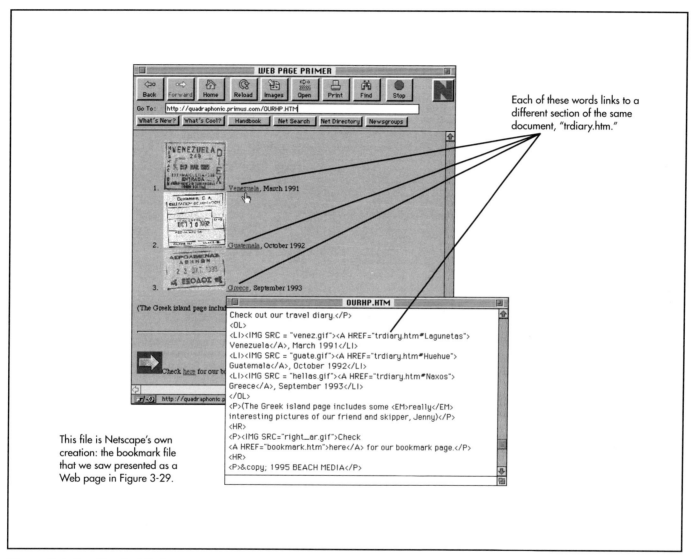

Each of these words links to a different section of the same document, "trdiary.htm."

This file is Netscape's own creation: the bookmark file that we saw presented as a Web page in Figure 3-29.

Figure 5-6: *Creating text links.*

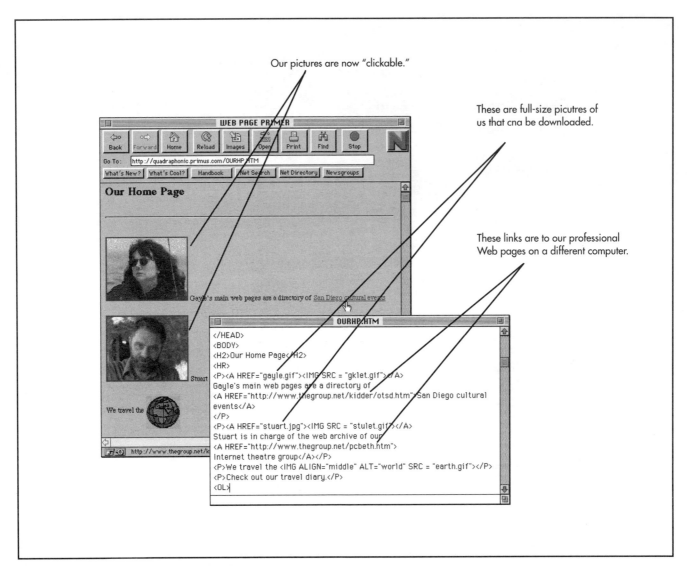

Figure 5-7: *Creating more complex links.*

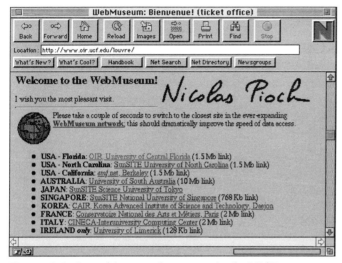

Figure 5-8: *Something caught our eye in the WebLouvre...*

Figure 5-9: *The little icon we decided to steal.*

<A NAME="Lagunetas">. Figure 5-6 shows the results.

Now, if we take a look at the top half of the page in Figure 5-7, we'll see that the in-line .GIFs themselves can be made into links. It's just a matter of wrapping the <A HREF="filename">Hyperlink Text</A> around everything correctly.

Note that the full-size "external" pictures can be any format, and many are in regular use on the Web. It explains why Netscape's Helper Applications box in the Preferences menu is so complicated.

How We Raided the Louvre... And They'll Never Catch Us!

Remember how we mentioned, back in Chapter 4, that the Web is a free-for-all that makes copyright attorneys wake up screaming in the night? And back in Chapter 2, the fact that the Louvre museum pages are renowned for good design? Put those two facts together and you have the background to a daringly successful raid we carried out on the Louvre one day.

We were wondering how to draw an icon to use as a link to our travel diary, when we came upon the Louvre page (depicted in Figure 5-8). "What a nice in-line .GIF," we thought. And then we thought, just as many art thieves must have thought, "Hmmm... would look swell in our collection." Figure 5-9 shows what we were after.

So we waited until the dead of night, Paris time (it helped that they were eight hours ahead), and then returned to that Web page. Moving silently but efficiently, we stroked our mouse pointer oh, so gently against that little picture we craved.

Working quickly now, afraid to hear the words *"mais, Monsieur, Madame... ooh la-la! Qu'est-ce que vous faites?"* we held down the mouse button a few seconds and brought up the menu shown in Figure 5-10, which gives away the name of the .GIF file and makes it so easy to commit the final act of larceny that it would seem a shame to let it escape. Another swift stroke of the mouse, and the prize was ours. All that remained was to decide, as Figure 5-11 shows, what to call our booty. We settled on the default **"earth.gif,"** and the rest you know.

Testing Your Page

As you can see, we've composed our page using nothing but a simple text editor, although if you decide to get serious about it you can get an HTML editor (see the sidebar that follows). The advantage of these programs is that they'll catch coding errors you might not otherwise see.

Fortunately, there's another handy way to check your code. If it's on a publicly available site, you can check it with the HTML Validation Service offered by Dan Connolly of Hal Computer Systems at

http://www.hal.com/~markg/WebTechs/validation-form/html

When you get to Dan's page, you just enter, in the box provided, the URL of the code you want checked, and it reports back any errors or inconsistencies it finds.

WebLint, another online HTML editing aid, will check any HTML document you've created for coding problems and let you know what you should do to fix them. Its address is

http://www.unipress.com/web-lint

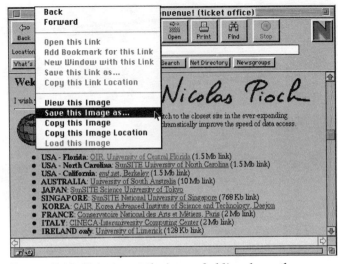

Figure 5-10: *Pointing at the image, holding down the mouse button a second or two allows us to grab it.*

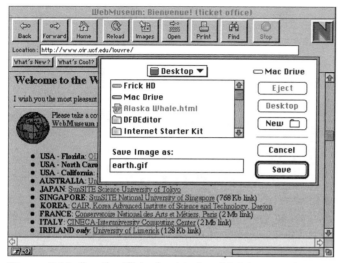

Figure 5-11: *"earth.gif" is about to be added to our private collection.*

If you intend to post your page for public access on the Web, it's important to remember that not everyone on the Web has Netscape. Netscape is very forgiving, but some other Web browsers can be very fussy. If at all possible, you should try viewing your page with other browsers (such as Mosaic and Cello). You should also consider the users without graphical interfaces who will see your page as pure text. You can test-view your page with the textual browser, Lynx, which you can access online. It's also a good idea to see what it looks like on different machines.

Of course, all of this is irrelevant if you've designed your page only for your own amusement and private use (and you can always send it to online friends). For truly professional Web page design, you should engage a professional. Accessing databases, devising proper forms for two-way information, and ensuring security is a whole 'nother kettle of fish.

Posting Your Page

So you think the whole world should know about the wonderful page you've just designed? The spirit of the Internet, after all, is that anyone can participate and there are no taste arbiters deciding who can and can't be part of it. Practically speaking, though, posting your page for public access is more complicated on the World Wide Web, unless you're hooked up to a major academic or big-business server—in which case all anyone needs is your URL address to get to your page.

If the nature of your page places it in the category of public service—information that other people might conceivably like to use—

you may find a community bulletin board or an access provider willing to post it free to enhance their own services.

If your page has a business or commercial aspect, there are plenty of access providers who would be happy to post it for you for a fee, and given the competitive nature of the business right now, the fees can be quite reasonable. Web business is a lively, developing field—check around and see what you can turn up.

Web Page Design Tips

Good Web page design is largely a matter of common sense. Nothing is more irritating to frequent travelers on the Web than coming across a huge document with multiple links and numerous in-line images that takes several minutes to download onto your system before you discover that it's not what you want at all.

Some useful things to remember:

- Close all your statements—every <X> needs a </X> with a few exceptions (such as <HR> and <IMG>).

- Keep your in-line images small—under 25k is a good guide. All six of the little in-line images we used in our demonstration page totalled less than 50k, and the page loads in a few seconds.

- Offer a link to larger images and if they're very large files (over 75k), tell readers how large they are.

Online HTML Editing Guides   Anyone interested in delving further into HTML composition can find lots of HTML guides and reference material on the Web. For the authoritative information, go straight to HTML's birthplace at the European Laboratory for Particle Physics (CERN), where the father of HTML himself, Tim Berners-Lee, has posted the HTML Style Guides, as well as a number of other HTML reference documents.

http://info.cern.ch/hypertext/WWW/Provider/Style/Overview.html

A good HTML FAQ can be found at:

http://sunsite.unc.edu/boutell/faq/www_faq.html

A couple of Mac-compatible HTML editors are obtainable by FTP. HTML SuperText and HTML.edit are both available at

ftp://ftp.ncsa.uiuc.edu/Mac/Mosaic/Helpers/ →

You can also create simple HTML documents online and save them to your own computer with the EasyHTML editor at

http://peachpit.ncsa.uiuc.edu:80/easyhtml/

Very recently (January 1995) a Macintosh version of the respected Windows HTML editor "HoTMetaL" was released. HoTMetaL Pro for Mac is by SoftQuad Inc. of Toronto. Contact SoftQuad for details at **hotmetal@sq.com**.

- Break large documents into smaller files logically. They'll load faster and be easier to use.
- Make sure your hyperlinks have full addresses.
- Test your page and all its links. If possible, test it with different browsers and on different kinds of machines.
- Describe your document accurately in the Title and resist the temptation to be too cute. The title is frequently used by Web searchers to find topics on the Web.
- Keep it simple. As in all good design, less is more.

Moving On

You may not realize it, but what you've actually learned in this chapter is HTML Plus, the newest version of the language of the Web (but not the last word—HTML 3 is on its way). With the simple basics we've given you we hope you'll have fun creating your own documents. If nothing else, it could be a great party piece—and perhaps slightly more entertaining than home videos of your latest trip (depending on your taste).

In the next chapter we'll talk about some of the more specialized Web applications. We'll dig into the wealth of reference materials available on the Web and toss up some of the more useful gems. We'll look at the various search engines and how you can find out what's available on the Web on any topic you're interested in. And finally, we'll give you some more neat pages you can visit as you continue your journeys on the Web with Netscape.

SPECIAL APPLICATIONS & SITES

Now that you've had a chance to see what the Web has to offer, you're probably eager to find your own particular interests—be they recreational, business or research-oriented. Finding that special something is not always an easy job, particularly because the Web changes every day.

Much of this chapter we'll devote to the task of searching the Web. We'll explain what kind of searches you can do and how to construct a search. Then we'll look at what some of our favorite search engines do and compare their results.

Then it's time for some more Web-sailing. We'll leave you with a list of our favorite Web sites—prize-winning pages, repositories of great information, or just-plain-fun stuff.

Web-Searching Tips

The first thing to realize about search engines on the Web is that not all searchers are created equal. The types of data they look for and the kinds of searches they do can be very different. One searcher may look for keywords in the titles of documents only, another will search all hypertext citation links in documents. Still a third will search the entire text of the documents in its base.

In the latter case, you can see how a lot of irrelevant information can be thrown up. This is especially so if the search is for a string instead of a word. Say you typed in "bee" for a keyword. If it's searching for the string, it will find "beer" and "has-been" and "beefcake" and who-knows-what-all.

Another difference in search engines is the extent to which they allow you to qualify your search, since obviously the more you can qualify it, the better your chances of getting exactly what you want. Most searchers encourage you to put as many keywords as you think relevant in your search, but this is not always helpful—it may simply turn up more irrelevant references than relevant ones.

Here are the basic types of searches possible. Bear in mind that not all searchers can do all of the various types of searches.

- Simple keyword search

  killer bee

This will return all documents containing either the word "killer" or "bee."

- Boolean query

  bee AND killer

This looks for occurrences of both words in a document, in any order.

- Phrase query

    "killer bee"

This will return all documents that contain "killer bee" as a phrase.

You can devise even more complex searches, such as

- Boolean queries with phrases

    "killer bee" AND California

- Simple structured query

    Title: "killer bee"

This will only return documents that have "killer bee" in the Title.

- Complex query

    California AND (Title: "killer bee")

No matter what you do, expect a few surprises. When we tried this out, our search for "killer bee" threw up, unexpectedly, a rock band called The Killer Bees and a NASA computer dubbed the killerbee.

The basic things to keep in mind when searching are:

- Know what kind of citations the searcher is looking for. Read the Help screens and FAQs before you start.

- Be as specific as you can.

- Use OR to widen your search. Use AND to narrow it.

- Don't use words that are too general or too common. The documentation for one Web searcher gives this example: "to be or not to be" is reduced to nothing by its initial keyword processing.

- Don't use plural forms or weird declensions.

- Realize that sometimes all it takes is a few good hits, as similar documents on a subject may well link to each other.

- Remember where you've been. Take notes if necessary.

Our Favorite Web Searchers

One of the most-thumbed sections of our bookmark list is the "Web Searchers" list. Like everyone else, we have research needs both formal (providing biology abstracts for non-Net-savvy clients) and informal (what was that address for the Paris Metro route planner?).

There are dozens of Web searchers available for your use, several of which you can find referenced on your Net Search directory button. To review our favorite searchers in some coherent way for this book, we gave them the task of searching for a commodity we love—French wine.

The WebCrawler

Possibly our favorite searcher because it's so easy and quick, the Crawler's at the University of Washington:

**http://webcrawler.cs.washington.edu/WebCrawler/
WebQuery.html**

(and you'd better get all those capital letters correct).

Figure 6-1 shows the Crawler's inquiry screen with that check box we love, to switch between an AND search and an OR search, plus the pull-down that limits the search if we just want a starting point rather than the full reference-desk treatment.

The Crawler does not search the Web itself when you ask it about French wine (or anything else, for that matter). Instead it searches its own index of the Web—a database of about 100mb which includes nearly 400,000 documents. Our one beef about the Crawler is that this index is not updated as often as we (and other Web citizens) would like. The massive update may happen only every three months, and a lot can happen in three months on the Web.

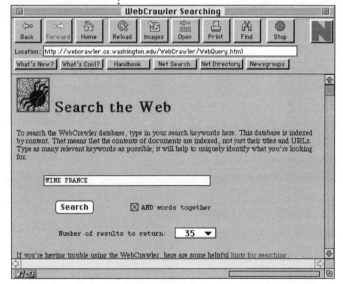

Figure 6-1: *Washington University's famous WebCrawler.*

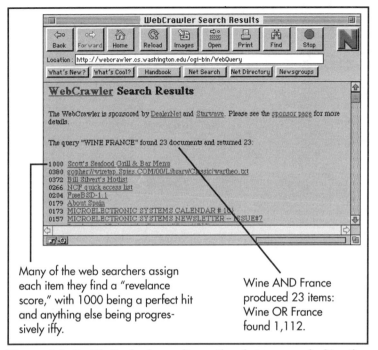

Many of the web searchers assign each item they find a "revelance score," with 1000 being a perfect hit and anything else being progressively iffy.

Wine AND France produced 23 items: Wine OR France found 1,112.

Figure 6-2: *Scott's Seafood wasn't exactly what we were looking for, but item 3 eventually led to gold.*

Harvest

There are two main URL addresses for the Harvest system: The first is more available and the second is more thorough.

http://www.town.hall.org/brokers/www-home-pages/query.html

http://harvest.cs.colorado.edu/brokers/www-home-pages/query.html

Why, you may ask, do they call themselves "brokers"? The answer is that these sites call in other searchers to aid them. The **town.hall** site uses a WAIS (Wide Area Information Service) indexer, which is efficient but weak when it comes to complex structured queries. The most powerful engine used is the Glimpse indexer at Arizona, which can even (sometimes) do a successful search on a misspelled keyword. Harvest's user-amicable features are its huge entry window and, especially, the format of its results lists. Our wine query produced 49 hits, of which this was the first:

1. filename: http://www.ifi.uio.no/~dash/wine/
   host: www.ifi.uio.no
   path: /~dash/wine/
   Description: The Wine project
   Content Summary

Everything underlined is a hypertext link, including that wonderful "Content Summary" that told us immediately that the "Wine project" was not the unfrozen concoction that helps us hang on but a software interface between Windows and UNIX X-11 systems. A typical Web-searching debacle, actually.

Lycos

http://lycos.cs.cmu.edu

The Washington WebCrawler was not only our favorite in terms of convenience, but also the best—until Lycos came along. Lycos—a whole array of hardware and software at Carnegie-Mellon University, Pittsburgh, is super-duper. Like the Crawler, it keeps its own local index for search speed, but it also fetches new documents "on the fly" and adds them into its ever-burgeoning indexes. The larger of the two principal catalogs indexed its millionth URL in November 1994.

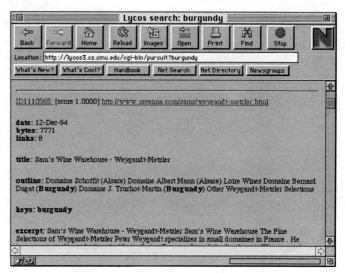

Figure 6-3: *Lycos gives us the story on Burgundy.*

Okay, Lycos is a little bit slower than the Crawler—but it is much more thorough. It found so many citations for French wine that we dared to test it on the focus of our personal wine interest: the Burgundy region of France. In less than a minute Lycos gave us 36 citations for "burgundy" (see Figure 6-3) and, in less than another minute, twelve more for "bourgogne." Neither Harvest nor the Worm had found anything on those keywords. Probably it helps that one of Carnegie-Mellon's computers is actually called burgundy.

Lycos has the interesting philosophy of scoring a citation higher if it comes up in the first paragraph of a document. It is also superior when it comes to Boolean and limited search strings. If you enter "bee." it will understand that you want only honey producers, not beetles, beefcakes or frisbees. It even allows "negative keyword" searching—so that, for instance, "ball -ball." would find "ballistic" but not "ball" itself.

World Wide Web Worm (WWWW)

http://www.cs.colorado.edu/home/mcbryan/WWWW.html

The Worm's big feature is its click-box that you can use to make a choice between searching hypertext, document titles, document names and substrings of URL addresses. It's one of the speediest searchers there is. And although it struck out on "burgundy," it was informative on wine more generally, even providing us with a wine map of Slovenia (some Slovenian has obviously invested hours in using the Web to promote the wines of the region—it's popped up several times).

The Worm claims technical superiority in its acceptance of so-called "regular expressions." These are not "regular" as opposed to "with all the trimmings, heavy on the mayo," but formatted strings containing things like "wildcards." DOS users know these because they use them for copying families of similarly named files, like *.TXT. In keyword searching, a wildcard can be as simple as an asterisk standing in for any string, such as 9*, meaning all ZIP Codes beginning with 9. The Worm's capabilities, however, go way beyond that and beyond the reach of most casual users of the Web.

The CUI W3 Catalog

http://cuiwww.unige.ch/w3catalog

CUI is very different from the other searchers we've chosen to feature in this chapter. It's almost like an index of abstracts—well, actually, that's exactly what it's like. Strange that it should have been the Centre Universitaire Informatique in Geneva that provided this, since it's virtually all in the English language. Its proximity to the region of Burgundy helps not at all when it comes to searching that keyword. But exhaustive Web searches are not CUI's game. Instead of searching the Web, it searches *indexes* of the Web, plagiarizing shamelessly the work of such toilers as Scott Yanoff and John December. The end result is a series of chatty little notations, each one providing a hypertext link to its source, which can be very useful indeed for certain levels of research.

The Great Burgundy Quest

This quick review was not a proper benchmark test, giving a hard-and-fast comparison of performance. We've tried, rather, to indicate what horses suit what courses and set up your expectations as well as possible.

You might wonder, though, what we finally came up with on burgundy wine. On wine, the Lycos hit-list, though accurate, actually did not lead to anything too interesting. Our best stuff came from picking the third item from the Crawler, Bill Silvert's Hotlist, and following that to the "Wine Home Page." That was nice but all-American, so we followed the link to "other wine pages" and ended up on the doorstep of our Net-buddy Gary "Gazza" Hunt, whose funky home page is shown in Figure 4-12 of this book. We already knew Gazza to be a wine buff and secretary of the wine society of the University of Bath, England. However, there was nothing immediately Burgundian at Bath so we followed Gazza's link back to the USA, to a wine newsletter called *GrapeVine*. That in turn offered a link to the archives of the USENET newsgroup "rec.food.drink," which in its turn offered yet another keyword search window, which finally produced seven good articles. Figure 6-4 shows the history list—another day, another Web site....

Example of a CUI Web Catalog Entry
October 14, 1994: <u>Forest Hill Vineyard</u> is now on the WWW. Forest Hill Vineyard is one of the most distinguished California vineyards, producing their award-winning chardonnay. Perfect for dinners, gifts, and to say 'congratulations' or 'I love you'. **(nwn)**

> **Note:** The link "<u>nwn</u>" takes you to NCSA What's New?—the same place you'll get to when using Netscape's What's New? directory button.

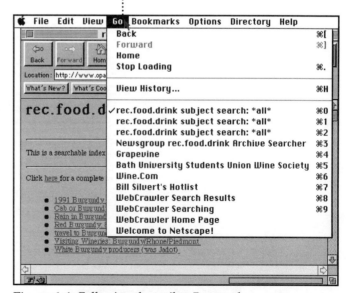

Figure 6-4: *Following the trail to Burgundy.*

Prize-Winning Web Pages

Web page design is fast becoming an art these days. How to balance visual presentation with good information and what kinds of information to include all need careful weighing. No doubt in your cruises so far you've found some good and bad examples and are beginning to form your own opinions on the subject.

Here are some of the winners of Web design contests, along with our own personal favorites. You'll find links to them all in our *Online Companion* at **http://www.vmedia.com/nqt.html**

Figure 6-5: *HotWired: Perhaps the best of the best in Web graphics—and they take advertising, too.*

The Best of the Web

This is the home of the annual Best of the Web Contest which awards Web page designers for outstanding presentations in more than a dozen categories. You'll find links to all the winners as well as runners-up here. It's a great place to see what the state of the art in Web design is these days.

http://wings.buffalo.edu/contest/awards/index.html

Global Network Navigator

O'Reilly & Associates, pioneers on the Web, present a wealth of resources on the Net on their extensive home pages, which include links to business pages, Net news, travel, personal finance—and their own picks of the best of the Web.

http://nearnet.gnn.com/gnn/gnn.html
Or go to **http://gnn.com** to become a registered subscriber.

ArtServe

Australian National University offers a comprehensive overview of their collections dealing with art history. Access to some 2,800 images of prints, from the 15th century to the 19th century, including some 2,500 images of classical architecture and sculpture from around the Mediterranean.
http://rubens.anu.edu.au/

London's Natural History Museum

A heavy-duty site but why not? It's one of the major museums in the world, the home of Charles Darwin and friends. Extensive information on the museum's science programs and collections on earth and life sciences and the flora and fauna of MesoAmerica, among other things.
http://www.nhm.ac.uk/

The Virtual Hospital

The University of Iowa hospital has put a considerable amount of patient information online here for public access. Get information about heart disease, poison control, obstetrics and gynecology, sexually transmitted diseases, and the warning signs of heart attack and stroke.
http://vh.radiology.uiowa.edu/IowaHealthBook/PatientInfo.html

Travels With Samantha

MIT programmer Phil Greenspun's travelogue of his trip around North America with his PowerBook, Samantha, won a Best of the Web '94 award, as much for his beautiful pictures as his personal travel narrative. Be forewarned that you'll need considerable memory to view his images.
http://www-swiss.ai.mit.edu/samantha/travels-with-samantha.html

The Constitution of the United States of America

Planning a Supreme Court battle? The entire Constitution is easily accessible online, thanks to Cornell University Law School.
http://www.law.cornell.edu/constitution/constitution.overview.html

Expo

Take a major museum tour on the Web via the virtual shuttle bus. Includes six expositions organized by the Library of Congress, with links to other major museum sites around the world. See the Soviet Archive Exhibit, the 1492 Exhibit, the Paleontology Exhibit, the Vatican Exhibit, the Dead Sea Scrolls Exhibit or the Spalato Exhibit of the palace of Diocletian at Split.
http://sunsite.unc.edu/expo/expo/busstation.html

Restaurant Le Cordon Bleu

The Restaurant Le Cordon Bleu is a side stop on the Expo tour above. A pictorial gourmet menu for each day of the week, with accompanying recipes from the cookbook *Le Cordon Bleu at Home*.
http://sunsite.unc.edu/expo/restaurant/restaurant.html
 If *haute cuisine* isn't your style, try a virtual eating experience at Fat Binary's Online Diner at
http://www.demon.co.uk:80/state51/fatb.html

The Virtual Tourist

Here you can find virtual tourist guides for countries around the world, as well as a link to a U.S. city guide index called City Net. Just click on the world map to see what's available.
http://wings.buffalo.edu/world/

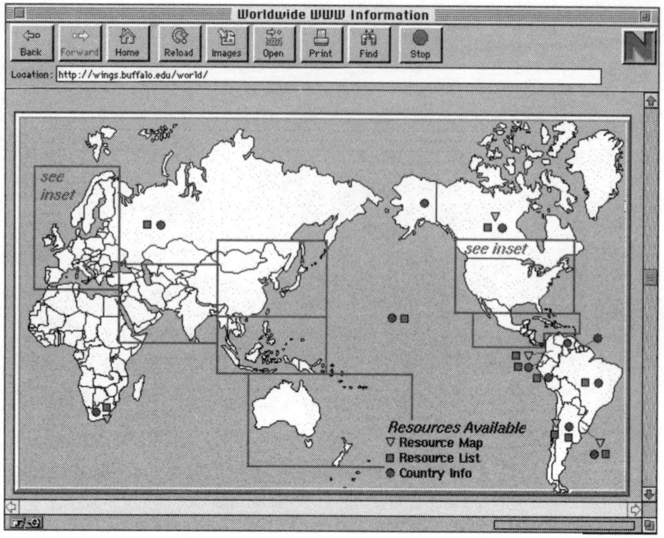

Welcome to the Globewide Network Academy

If you can earn a degree by mail these days, why not by e-mail? This unique site is the first cyberuniversity, a project by a consortium of educational and research organizations dedicated to devising a complete online university.
http://uu-gna.mit.edu:8001/uu-gna/

Arctic Adventours, Inc.

This Norwegian tour company advertises their expeditions to the Arctic area aboard the yacht Arctic Explorer at this site. Lots of stunning pictures of Northern Norway, Siberia and anonymous icebergs.
http://www.oslonett.no/data/adv/AA/AA.html

The Branch Mall

The Branch Mall is one of the largest and longest established Internet Malls, with wares ranging from flowers and tee shirts to computer parts. Branch's success has been featured in the *New York Times, Inc Magazine, Money* and on PBS Television.
http://www.branch.com:1080/index.html

Figure 6-6: *If only travel were this easy...nah, the agony's half the fun.*

The Hypertext Webster

An online searchable index of Webster's dictionary. Look up any word and get the definition. If you spell it wrong, it will guess at what you mean and prompt you. Definitions are themselves hypertext linked.
http://c.gp.cs.cmu.edu:5103/prog/webster?/

Current Weather Maps/Movies

The definitive site for weather maps and information. Find out the weather anywhere in the world and view the latest satellite pictures.
http://clunix.cl.msu.edu:80/weather/

The Electronic Frontier Foundation

The Electronic Frontier Foundation is a non-profit civil liberties, public-interest organization working to protect freedom of expression, privacy and access to online resources and information. For serious discussions of these developing issues, go to
http://www.eff.org/

Paris

A perfect companion to Le WebLouvre, this is a complete visitor's guide to Paris—its museums, monuments, special expositions, cafes, restaurants and sights, as well as practical information like air and rail transportation, the metro and hotels. Lots of swell images.
http://meteora.ucsd.edu:80/~norman/paris/

Sliding Tiles Puzzles

Remember those little hand-held sliding tile puzzles? Here's the computer version, a collection which includes basic geometrics and celebrity faces. The sliding tile puzzle seems to be very popular on the Net.
http://www.cm.cf.ac.uk/User/Andrew.Wilson/Puzzle/collection.html

The Virtual Radio

Hear the latest in new music here. Choose which song you'd like to hear and download it right to your machine in a radio-quality broadcast of the entire cut. Each page contains band information, a description of the band's music, and sometimes images of the band. Beware: with names like the Guttersluts, Fire Rooster and Metallingus, this is not elevator music.
http://www.microserve.net:80/vradio/

Fairy Tales

Not an HTML document but a wonderful repository where you can download the complete text of your favorite fairy tales—*Aladdin, Beauty and the Beast, Ali Baba and the Forty Thieves, The Emperor's New Clothes, Hansel and Gretel, The Pied Piper of Hamelin, The Seven Voyages of Sinbad*, and other stories you haven't thought about for years.
gopher://ftp.std.com:70/11/obi/book/Fairy.Tales/Grimm

alt.binaries made EZ

Every day brings a hundred or so new pieces of computer art, from space pictures to "my wife streaking a hotel corridor" (we're not making this up, folks). Even if you have one of the super newsreaders that downloads and uudecodes them hands-off, the problem still is decid-

ing what's worth your time. This French Web page provides a buffet of all the latest, on a pick 'n' click basis.
http://web.cnam.fr/Images/Usenet/

Icon Browsers

There are so many icon browsers out there that we are forced to suspect that it's one of the tasks comp. sci. professors give their promising students as a UNIX programming exercise. Who cares? The results are greatly beneficial to the Web community at large. Copyright be damned—what's the point of 100,000 of us all laboring to create the same arrows and buttons? Here's our current favorite:
http://www.di.unipi.it/iconbrowser/icons.html

This hat FOR SALE.

Figure 6-7: *Light relief.*

The Global Village Idiot

There had to be one, didn't there? The Idiot claims to be "a welcome break from the Propeller-Heads that inhabit the majority of the Net" and warns that "if you have come here for Intellectual Challenge or Thoughtful Discourse, you are in the wrong place." Meet other villagers, visit the village shops and even dress like the Idiot (you can buy his hat).
http://www.primenet.com/~hanibal/index.html

URouLette

Don't know where you want to go? Let URouLette choose for you. Spin the wheel and you'll be sent off to a random Web address. No guarantees.
http://ukanaix.cc.ukans.edu:80/cwis/organizations/ kucia/uroulette/uroulette.html

Moving On

So now you've done it. You've learned to navigate the Web with Netscape Navigator, and you've taken some interesting cruises across the fast-changing waters of the World Wide Web. Congratulations! You can now say, "I'm ready for my future, Mr. DeMille."

Having seen what you've seen, you're probably wondering, "What is the future anyway?" A few things are certain: the Web will get bigger, it will be easier to access, and a lot more people will be participating in it. But lots of things are unknown. Who will pay for its development? How much will it all cost? What kinds of businesses will grow out of it? How will it affect our lives?

Businesses large and small, academic institutions and governments will all have a say in this, but so will each one of us who uses it. The Internet continues to be the most revolutionary democratic forum to come along in hundreds of years.

You too qualify as a fully endowed cybercitizen. Care to venture an opinion?

APPENDIX A
UNDOCUMENTED FEATURES OF NETSCAPE NAVIGATOR

Whether "undocumented features" are undocumented because somebody forgot to mention some brilliant piece of code to the technical writing department, or because nobody thought we'd be interested, is a matter of debate. The fact is that all software has a few features that aren't noted in the manual. Netscape is too new for a complete list to exist, but here are some we've discovered or heard about on the Netscape grapevine.

Different Strokes for Different Folks

Keyboard alternatives for common commands:

- Delete acts like PgUp.
- Spacebar acts like PgDn.
- ⌘C performs an Edit/Copy.
- ⌘V performs an Edit/Paste.
- ⌘X performs an Edit/Cut.
- If you hold down the Option key while loading a URL, it will load to disk instead of the screen.

- If you hold down the Option key while including Web page text in the e-mail window, it will be included without the ">" at the beginning of every line.

What Does the N Do?

The logo is an active link: Click on it and go to the Netscape Communications Corporation's home page.

Who Was That Masked Programmer?

The pseudo-URL **about:** does a few interesting things—the most interesting being the form **about:authors** which brings you a list of Netscape programmers, indicating roughly who did what. We assume Lou Montulli was left on his own in the lab one night, because earlier versions of Netscape also reacted to the URL "montulli:" They've put a stop to that, but not to the shortcut to Lou's favorite project—the fishcam, which gives you "quasi-live" camera angles on the Netscape aquarium. Hit Control-Option F to see fish behavior, and possibly also catch the reflection of Lou Montulli in the front glass. Of course, on days when Lou comes to the office in his Hawaiian shirt, you may not even know you're seeing him!

Netscape's House Organ

The URL **http://home.netscape.com/people/** brings Netscape Communications Corporation's staff list into your content window. Many of them have home pages you can browse, and practically all have clickable mail links. You can even offer a contribution to Netscape's internal zine.

Secure Pages to Order

As we mentioned back in Chapter 3, there are not yet many secure pages on the Web. Even the CIA's pages (**http://www.ic.gov**) aren't secure, for heaven's sake!

If you're curious to know what a secure page looks like, go to any of the Netscape Communications Corporation's own pages—the Welcome page, for instance. Now put a cursor in the URL window and change "**http://**" to "**https://**" Reload the page, and you'll have the pleasure of seeing that broken key in the lower left corner mend itself, and the blue color bar appear between the directory buttons and the content area.

GIF Retrieval

Browse the files in your cache subdirectory. Some of them will turn out to be images which Netscape saved in your temporary directory. Rename them as .GIF files to save them permanently.

Hypertext Newsgroup Reading

Certain versions of Netscape have no View All Newsgroups button (as depicted in Figure 4-15). You can nevertheless produce the big newsgroup file by entering **news:*** in the URL window. The newsgroup names come up as hypertext links enabling you to go to any group you like the look of. Or you can copy a newsgroup name onto the Clipboard, then paste it into the "Subscribe" window. The * can be used as a "wild card" in newsgroup names, too. For example, **news:alt.*** will bring up all of the alt. newsgroups.

APPENDIX B
COMMON NETSCAPE ERROR MESSAGES

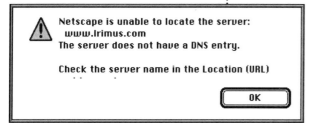

Netscape is unable to locate the server:
www.lrimus.com
The server does not have a DNS entry.

Check the server name in the Location (URL)

OK

Unable to locate the server

This can arise from an erroneous URL, a disconnect or the absence (perhaps temporary) of the requested site. Check your URL carefully.

Not found

This error comes up when you follow a link to a URL that no longer exists.

404 Not found

The URL you have provided does not exist. Check the syntax carefully.

403 Forbidden

You're trying to visit a Web site that you or your server has no permission to access.

Connection refused by host

Although this one sounds the same as "Forbidden," it's more likely to be a temporary refusal. What it's saying is that the host address does actually exist but it's not available right now. Down for maintenance, most likely. Try later.

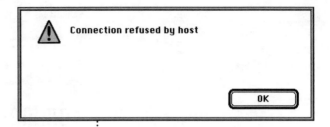

Helper application not found

Your Preferences/Helper Applications dialog box refers to a helper that Netscape cannot locate in your computer. This error is thrown up when you are attempting to download a file of the type handled by the helper. Note the extension of the file you're downloading and go to the dialog box to see what Netscape's trying to find.

File contains no data

The URL you requested has been found but it is null. This error can sometimes be remedied by appending the port number ":80"

Too many users

You've hit a very popular site that has the maximum allowable number of visitors already.

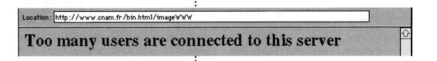

Bad File Request

This arises when you submit a form that is in some way invalid. It can also arise from erroneous HTML coding at the site you are on. Not much you can do about that!

TCP error encountered while sending request to server.

Network data error. Try later. If persistent, contact your sysadmin.

Failed DNS lookup

The DNS software at your access provider's site was not able to convert a URL you requested to a valid IP address. Check the spelling and format of the URL.

NNTP Server error

Make sure you have the NNTP host entered correctly in the Preferences dialog box. If the NNTP host is correct, most likely your news server is down or congested. Try later.

Cannot add form submission result to bookmark list

When you submit a form page and get an answer page back—as, for example, when you use a Web crawler to search for a keyword—the answer page is not a legitimate URL and so cannot be made into a bookmark. Look at the URL string and somewhere you'll see "cgi-bin." Any time you see that as part of a URL you'll know this is a nonsavable answer page.

APPENDIX C
ABOUT THE ONLINE COMPANION

Netscape into the World Wide Web! The *Netscape Online Companion* is an informative tool, as well as an annotated software library. It aids in your exploration of the World Wide Web while at the same time supporting and enhancing the Netscape Web Browser. Sections of *Netscape Quick Tour*, the hard-copy book, are reproduced and hyperlinked to the exciting WWW sites and tools that they reference. So you can just click on the name of the reference and jump directly to the site you are interested in.

Perhaps one of the most impressive features of the *Netscape Online Companion* is its Software Archive. Here, you'll find and be able to download the latest versions of all the software mentioned in *Netscape Quick Tour* that are freely available on the Internet. This software ranges from Netscape helper applications such as GifConverter, Sound Machine and Sparkle, which enhance Netscape's graphics and sound capabilities, to many of your basic Internet essentials such as Eudora, an e-mail manager, and Fetch, which allows you to transfer files easily to and from your computer. Also, with Ventana Online's helpful description of the software, you'll know exactly what you're getting and why—so you won't download the software only to find you have no use for it.

The *Netscape Online Companion* also links you to the Ventana Library, where you'll find useful press and jacket information on a variety of Ventana offerings. Plus, you have access to a wide selection of exciting new releases and coming attractions. In addition, Ventana's Online Library allows you to order the books you want.

The *Netscape Online Companion* represents Ventana Online's ongoing commitment to offering the most dynamic and exciting products possible. And soon Ventana Online will be adding more services, including more multimedia supplements, searchable indexes and sections of the book reproduced and hyperlinked to the Internet resources they reference.

To access, connect via the World Wide Web to
http://www.vmedia.com/nqtw.se.html

GLOSSARY

Alias   A type of nickname used, for example, in e-mail managers so that you can enter "fred" and your e-mail manager knows you mean **edf556@froward.cursci.com**.

Anchor   In hypertext, the object that is highlighted and "clickable." It may be a word, a phrase, or an inline image.

Anonymous FTP   An FTP service that serves any user, not just those who have accounts at the site. Anonymous FTP generally permits downloading of all files but uploading only into a directory called "/ incoming."

Archie   A keyword search service that searches the directory and file titles of all FTP sites that are indexed.

ASCII   American Standard Code for Information Interchange: An agreed-upon coding of letters, numbers and symbols. An ASCII file is one which makes use of only the first 128 ASCII symbols—the symbols you see on your keyboard, basically. The advantage of ASCII files is that one bit per byte is always available for purposes such as error-checking.

.AU   In hypermedia, an audio file format common in DOS systems.

Backbone   The connections between the primary computers in a network. Stub networks branch off the backbone.

Bandwidth   Used (somewhat inaccurately) to express the maximum possible throughput of a data link in bits per second. A so-called T1 line has a bandwidth of 1.544 Mbps.

Binary   A numbering system used in computing, which has 2 as its base. A binary file, as opposed to an ASCII file, makes use of 256 symbols and so does not keep a bit free for error-checking.

BinHex   A type of file conversion used for transmitting Macintosh executable files. BinHex essentially turns a compressed binary file into an ASCII file for transmission. Upon arrival, the file is "un-BinHexed."

Bookmark   Web address in the form of a URL that a user keeps a record of in order to be able to return to it easily.

Cache   1. An area of RAM set aside to hold data or instructions that would normally be read from disk, in order to speed up access to it. 2. In network operation, an area of disk set aside to hold data that would normally be read from the Net, for the same reason. Netscape makes use of both types of cache.

Client/server software   An arrangement of computers, very common in Internet systems, whereby a small system called the client makes use of the data management services of a much larger computer, the server. Netscape Navigator is a client/server system, with the client running on your machine taking advantage of the far greater processing power of the server at a remote site.

Content window   The portion of the Netscape screen in which actual page content is seen, as opposed to the control and information portions.

Cyberspace   Fanciful term coined by William Gibson in the novel *Neuromancer* to describe the sum total of computer-accessible information in the world.

Dial-up account   The type of Internet access account that is connected only when a modem connection is established, as distinct from a direct permanent connection. This is often used to refer to a shell account as opposed to a SLIP- or PPP-type access, even though SLIP/PPP accounts are frequently also established by dial-up.

Direct connection   A hard-wired connection between a computer and the Internet, giving that computer an IP address and the ability to function as a Web site.

DNS (Domain Name Server)   Software that converts host names to IP addresses.

Eudora   A popular e-mail manager developed by Qualcomm Inc. of San Diego.

.EXE file extension   In DOS, denotes an "executable" file that will run if its name is simply entered at the DOS prompt (with or without the .EXE). Files that are executable in Windows frequently have the extension .EXE also.

External image   An image that may be accessed by a hypertext link from an HTML page but is not automatically displayed when the page loads, as is an in-line image.

FAQ (Frequently Asked Questions)   Pronounced "fak," shorthand for an information file about answering the most commonly posed questions about a program or newsgroup. You should always read the FAQ first to avoid repeating questions answered there.

Fetch   Name of a very convenient FTP application for Macintosh.

Finger   Originally a UNIX command requesting information about another registered UNIX account-holder. Now available to Netscape by courtesy of Finger "gateways."

Flame   A deliberately abusive message in e-mail or USENET post.

FTP (File Transfer Protocol)   One of the original protocols on the Internet, which allows for very efficient transfer of entire data files between computers but discourages interactive browsing.

.GIF (Graphics Interchange Format)   One of many formats for computerized images, designed to be highly transportable between computer systems. Almost invariably used for in-line images in Web pages.

Gopher   An Internet search-and-display application that reduces all Internet resource "trees" to onscreen menus.

Greek   In desktop publishing, an approximate representation of text used when there is insufficient screen space to show it in properly readable form. By extension, any onscreen text that is garbled.

Helper applications   Applications that cooperate with Netscape and other Web browsers to perform functions that Netscape itself is not programmed to perform , such as viewing video files.

Home page   1. The page you designate (in the Preferences/Styles dialog box) as the Web page you want Netscape to load at startup. 2. A personal page you control and refer other people to.

Host   A computer whose primary function is facilitating communications.

Hotlist   A personal list of favorite Web addresses, organized so that it creates hypertext links to the addresses. Same as a bookmark list.

HTML (HyperText Markup Language)   A convention for inserting "tags" into a text file that Web browsers such as Netscape can interpret to display or link to hypermedia.

HTML+   A more rigorous version of HTML, allowing for a wider range of media effects.

Hypermedia   Media such as video and audio, which go beyond what was thought (not so very long ago!) to be the realm of personal computer display.

Hypertext   System of interactive text linking allowing the reader to choose any path through the sum total of available text.

In-line image   On a Web page, an image intended to be loaded along with the page text (although in-lines can be suppressed by a Netscape user to speed up page-loading).

Internet   A network of computer networks stretching across the world, linking computers of many different types. No one organization has control of the Internet or jurisdiction over it.

IP address   An Internet machine address formatted with just numbers rather than a host name. An IP address may also contain a port number, separated from the host address by a colon.

.JPEG (Joint Photographic Experts Group)   A modern image file format allowing for a choice of three levels of file compression, with progressive trade-off of image quality.

Killer app   A highly successful, popular and much-acclaimed computer application.

Link   In the World Wide Web context, short for "hypertext link," meaning a path a user may follow that connects one part of a document to another part of the same document, a different document or some other resource.

Lynx   Name of a text-only World Wide Web browser, available for UNIX, Linux, DOS and a few other operating systems.

Mail server   A computer whose primary function is e-mail management for a group of subscribers.

MacTCP   The most common TCP/IP stack used on Macintosh computers.

MIME (Multipurpose Internet Mail Extensions)   A set of agreed-upon formats enabling binary files to be sent as e-mail or attached to e-mail. "MIME types" have come to mean hypermedia formats in general, even when not communicated by e-mail.

Mirror site   A subsidiary FTP site that has the same content as the main site it reflects. Used to take the load off sites so popular that they are frequently inaccessible because of congestion.

Mosaic   A World Wide Web graphical browser, forerunner of Netscape Navigator.

Mozilla   Pet name the software's authors gave to Netscape Navigator during its development.

.MPEG (Motion Picture Experts Group)   Modern standard format for compression and storage of video hypermedia files.

NCSA (National Center for Supercomputing Applications)   A U.S. Government center at the University of Illinois. NCSA developed the Mosaic Web browser and other Internet interfaces.

NEWSRC file   A data file that keeps a record of what newsgroups a user is subscribed to and which articles have already been read.

Newsreader   Software whose function is to interact with USENET newsgroups, providing services such as subscription, display, follow-up, print, download and so on.

NNTP (Network News Transport Protocol)   The protocol used by the USENET newsgroups to disseminate bulletins.

Nuntius   A popular Macintosh newsreader for USENET newsgroups.

Packet-switching   A system, used extensively throughout the Internet for handling messages based upon the breakdown of a message into standardized packets, each of which is independently routed to the addressee.

POP mail (Post Office Protocol)   An e-mail system which establishes your primary mailbox in your own desktop computer rather than at your access provider's site.

PPP (Point-to-Point Protocol)   A convention for transmitting packet-switched data.

Proxy   Device used to access the Internet around a "fire wall" put up to ensure security in a large system.

QuickTime   A hypermedia video format, invented for Macintosh multimedia systems but now also available for DOS/Windows.

Search engine   Keyword-searching algorithm or complete software package including search algorithms.

Server   The server half of a client/server pair: the computer that handles the primary data management tasks on behalf of its clients.

Shell   A simple, usually menu-driven, interface that shields a computer user from the complexities of operating systems such as UNIX. Hence a common type of Internet connection, known as a "UNIX shell account," can be operated efficiently with extremely limited actual knowledge of UNIX.

SLIP (Serial Line Internet Protocol)   A convention for transmitting packet-switched data.

Socket   One of a series of memory addresses in a computer reserved for data exchange with a TCP/IP stack.

Source document   In the World Wide Web, the raw file that an HTML author creates, as distinct from a Web page, which is a representation of a source document in hypertext.

Stack   In the context of TCP/IP, the ordered series of protocols and packet drivers required to interface a desktop computer with the Internet.

Tag   Name given to the code strings embedded in HTML documents, such as <H1>.

TCP/IP (Transmission Control Protocol/Internet Protocol)   Shorthand for the most common packet-switching protocols used on the Internet.

TELNET   A software system that establishes a connection between two computers for the purpose of data exchange. Unlike FTP, TELNET is interactive and, as commonly used, makes a desktop computer behave as though it were the workstation of a much larger computer.

.TIFF   (Tagged Image File Format)   A standard format for storing hypermedia image files. A .TIFF file is uncompressed (and therefore generally large) and can contain many images.

UNIX   The operating system of choice for computers dedicated to the Internet. UNIX is inherently suited to network operations.

URL (Universal Resource Locator)   An address that completely defines a resource of the World Wide Web. A URL has four elements:

- The service—http or ftp or a few others.
- The host—the computer that handles the resource.
- The port number (often necessary because it defaults according to the service requested).
- The path and filename of the resource.

Format of a URL is **service://host:port/path**.

Usenet   A worldwide network exchanging news bulletins grouped under subject categories called "newsgroups." Most newsgroups are open, and anyone may contribute. Netscape has its own built-in newsreader for interacting with USENET.

WAIS (Wide Area Information Service)   A database service of the Internet allowing structured searching for keyword combinations. WAIS supplies a measure of how well documents it finds match your keywords, in the form of a relevance score. A score of 1,000 would indicate a perfect match.

.WAV   A standard format for storing hypermedia audio files.

Web   Short for the World Wide Web.

Web browser   User interface to the Web. Netscape is a graphical Web browser.

Web crawler   Software that searches the Web (or, more commonly, a database derived from the Web) for keywords input by a user.

Web page   Coherent document that is readable by a Web browser. A Web page may vary in complexity all the way from a simple piece of text enclosed by the HTML tags <PRE>....</PRE>, meaning "pre-formatted," to a densely coded HTML file giving the user access to many types of hypermedia.

Web server   A server computer equipped to offer World Wide Web access to its clients.

Web spider   A type of keyword search software.

Webmaster   Person at a Web server site who is qualified to administer all Web resources at that site.

World Wide Web   Arrangement of Internet-accessible resources including hypertext and hypermedia, addressed by URLs.

Zine   An online magazine.

INDEX

A

About: authors 126
About Netscape option 44
About the Internet option 44
Add Bookmark option 40
Addresses
    See URL addresses
alt.binaries Made EZ 122–23
American Memory Project 74
Archie 85–87
Arctic Adventours, Inc. 120
Art Web sites 72, 118, 122–23
ArtServe 118
Audio files 67–68
    preferences 21
    size 67
    Virtual Radio 122
    See also Helper applications
Auto load images option 41

B

Back
    menu option 38
    toolbar button 23, 29
Background (screen) 57, 62
Backing up 23, 29, 38
Bad File Request (error message) 130
Best of the Web 117

Big Dummy's Guide 44
BinHex 13
    installing StuffIt 19
Boardwatch 70
Bookmark lists
    customizing for multiple users 61
    deleting 53
    displaying single categories 54
    grouping in categories 51–52
    heading categories 52–53
    indenting 53
    managing multiple 55
    organizing 51–54
    saving 55
    separating categories 53
    viewing 40
    viewing headers only 54
Bookmarks 50–55
    creating 40, 51
    e-mail correspondents 80
    exporting 55
    FTP sites 81
    importing 55
    making your home page 54
Bookmarks menu 40
Boolean searching 110
Branch Mall 120
Brokers 113
Browsers of Web 6
    defined 10
Business Web sites 75–76

C

Cache
  alotting memory/space   58
  refreshing from   29–30, 37
Cannot add form submission result...(error message)   131
Cardiff Movie Database Browser   77
Census (U.S.) Web site   76
Centre Universitaire Informatique   115–16
Clipboard
  copying to   36–37
  sending contents as e-mail   35
Close option   36
Colors
  links   56–57
  preferences   57
Commercial Web sites   75–76
Connecting to Internet   12–14
  problems   22
Connection refused by host (error message)   130
Connolly, Dan   104
Constitution of the United States   119
Copy option   36–37
Copying
  to Clipboard   36–37
  text longer than one screen   37
Copyright information   44
Creating Web services
  See HTML
CUI W3 Catalog   115–16
Curry School   73

D

Database Web sites   76–77
Deleting bookmarks   53
Dictionaries on Web   121
Directories
  listing   43, 46
  searching   85–87

Directory buttons   22–23, 45–47
  clearing from screen   41
  displaying   41
Directory menu   42–44
Dissecting online   73–74
Document Information option   35
Downloading Netscape   14–18
  Fetch   15–16
  FTP dial-up account   16–18
  mirror sites   13
  UNIX operating system   18

E

Edit menu   36–37
Educational Web sites   73–74, 120
Electronic Frontier Foundation   121
Electronic publications   70
E-mail   79–80
  bookmarks of correspondents   80
  Clipboard contents   35
  mailto: 80
  preferences   21
  problems   80
  sending   34–35
  server   58
Entertainment Web sites   77
Error messages   129–31
  See also Problems
Exiting
  See Quitting
Exploratorium   72
Expo   119
Export bookmarks option   55
External images   65

F

Failed DNS lookup (error message)   131
Fairy Tales   122

FAQs (Frequently Asked Questions)
   menu option   44
   Web-related information   89
Feedback to Netscape   45, 69
Fetch
   acquiring   13–14
   downloading Netscape   15–16
File contains no data (error message)   130
File menu   32–36
Files
   dealing with different types   60
   displaying info about   41
   extensions   93
   listing   17
   loading into Netscape   33, 93
   temporary   59
   types   64–68
   See also specific types of files
Find button   31
Finding
   See Searching
Finger   87–88
Fire walls   60
Fonts   57
Forms   68–69
Forward
   menu option   39
   toolbar button   29
403 Forbidden (error message)   129
404 Not Found (error message)   129
Frequently Asked Questions
   See FAQs
FTP   80–81
   displaying file information   41
   downloading Netscape   16–18
   helper application site   83
   sites list in bookmarks   81

G

Genetic databases   77
.GIF files   64–65, 97–100
   See also Images
Glimpse indexer   113
Global Network Navigator   117
Global Village Idiot   123
Globewide Network Academy   120
Go menu   38–39
Go to Newsgroups option   43
Gopher   82
Gopher Jewels   82
Governmental Web sites   74–75, 119
Graphics
   See Images

H

Handbook
   directory button   23, 46
   menu option   44
Harvest   113
Hawaii (Web site)   78
Headers (bookmarks)
   adding   52–53
   viewing list   54
Health Web sites   118
Help menu   44–45
Help (online manual)   23, 44, 46
Helper Application Not Found (error message)   130
Helper applications
   preferences   21, 59–60
   TELNET   59, 83
   See also Audio files; Images; Video files
History list
   navigating   29, 38–39
   viewing   39
Home
   menu option   39
   toolbar button   29

Home pages
    creating
        See HTML
    directory   78–79
    making bookmarks into   54
    marking for revisiting
        See Bookmarks
    posting on Web   105–6
    returning to   29, 39
    setting   25, 56
Hotwired   70
    graphics   117
How to Create Web Services option   45
How to Get Support option   45
How to Give Feedback option   45
HTML (HyperText Markup Language)   6
    defined   9
    viewing   91–92
HTML files
    adding images   97–100
    adding links   100–103
    copying from other sites   103–4
    creating   93–105
    design tips   106–7
    editors   104, 106
    loading into Netscape   33
    posting on Web   105–6
    testing   104–5
    validation service   104
HTML tags   92–96
Http (URL address)   79
Human Genome Project   77
Hypermedia   5, 9
Hypertext   4–5
    defined   9
HyperText Markup Language
    See HTML
Hypertext Webster   121

I

Icon Browsers   123
Icons
    audio files   68
    browsers   123
    missing image   41
Images
    calling into HTML files   97–100
    displaying/downloading   30, 37, 41, 59
    enlarging   24
    external   65
    file types   64–66
    icon for missing   41
    in-line   65, 97–100
    manipulating   97
    saving   66, 127
    scanning   97
    screen background   57, 62
    toolbar button   30
    viewing   21, 60, 65–66
        using text viewers   97, 100
Import bookmarks option   55
Indenting bookmark lists   53
In-line images   65, 97–100
Installing Netscape   20
Interesting Business Sites   76
Internet
    connecting to
        See Connecting to Internet
    defined   2, 9
    finding other users   87–88
    general information   44
    how it works   3
    new resources   42, 45
Internet Business Center   76
Internet Directory option   43
Internet Search option   43
Internet White Pages   43

J

Japanese language   57–58
.JPEG files   64–66
JPEGView   21, 60, 65–66, 97

K

Keyboard alternatives   125–26
Keyword searching   110
      negative   114

L

Launching Netscape   22–23
Library of Congress Web site   119
License agreement   22
Links
      color changes   56–57
      creating in HTML   100–103
      defined   56–57
      displaying URLs   49
      following   5, 23
Load Images option   37
Loading
      local files into Netscape   33, 93
      stopping   31, 39
      viewing progress   49
Local mode   33, 93
Logo
      link to Netscape   126
      pulsating   50
London Guide   77–78
London's Natural History Museum   118
Louvre Museum
      See WebMuseum, Paris
Lycos   114
Lynx   100

M

MacTCP   13
Magazines on Web   70
Mail Document option   34–35
Mail server   58
Mailto: 80
Menu bar   32–45
      Bookmarks menu   40
      Directory menu   42–44
      Edit menu   36–37
      File menu   32–36
      Go menu   38–39
      Help menu   44–45
      Options menu   40–42
      View menu   37–38
Mirror sites   13
Mosaic   8–9
      compared to Netscape   8
Mother Jones   70
Mouse   46–47
Movie Studios   77
Movies
      See Video files
Mozilla   6
.MPEG files   66–67
Multiple users   55, 61
Multitasking   32, 59
Museums on Web   72–73, 118
Music sites   122

N

NASA   75
Negative keywords   114
Net directory button   46
Net Search directory button   46
Netscape
      acquiring   13–14
      capabilities   7–8
      compared to Mosaic   8

customizing for multiple users 61
defined 10
history 8–9
online manual 23, 44, 46
programmers 126
quitting 36
registering 22
release notes 44
requirements for running 12–14
undocumented features 125–27
unpacking 19
update information 88–89
Netscape Communications Corporation 8–9
favorite pages 42, 46
Internet address 17
staff list 126
Netscape Galleria 43
NETSCAPE.INI file 61
New Window option 32
News Web sites 71
Newsgroups 83–85
accessing 43, 46, 83
browsing names 84, 127
directory button 46
preferences 21, 58
server address 58
subscribing 84
threaded articles 84
unsubscribing 84–85
viewing article titles 84
Web-related information 90
Newspapers on Web 71
NEWSRC file 83
NNTP Server error (error message) 131
Not Found (error message) 129

O

On Security option 44
Open button 30
Open File option 33

Open Location option 32
Open Market Inc. 75
Options menu 40–42

P

Page Setup option 35–36
Pages 6–7
browsing 23, 29, 38–39
creating
        See HTML
defined 6, 9
going directly to
        See URL addresses
good design examples 117–23
history of specific 35
marking for revisiting
        See Bookmarks
printing setup 35–36
refreshing 29–30, 37
viewing next 29, 39
viewing previous 23, 29, 38
See also Home pages
Paris 121
PC Magazine 70
PC Week 70
Phrase searching 111
PostScript file 36
PPP (Point-to-Point Protocol) 12
Preferences 20–21, 56–60
colors 57
helper applications 59–60
images 59
menu option 40–42
newsgroups 58
saving 42
screen appearance 56
security 59–60
styles 56–57

Print
    menu option   36
    toolbar button   31
Printer setup   31, 36
Printing   31, 36
    page setup   35–36
    source code   31
    window larger than page   36
Problems
    connecting   22
    e-mail   80
    full page not printing   36
    page appearance   29–30, 37
    URL failure   48
    See also Error messages
Programmers   126
Programming
    See HTML
Progress bar   49
Proxies   60
Puzzles, Sliding Tiles   122

Q

QuickTime   66–67
Quitting Netscape   36

R

Refreshing pages   29–30, 37
Registering Netscape   22
Regular expressions   115
Release Notes option   44
Relevance score   113
Reload
    menu option   37
    toolbar button   29–30
Restaurant Le Cordon Bleu   119
Running Netscape   22–23

S

Save As option   33
Save Next Link As option   34
Save Options   42
Saving
    bookmark lists   55
    images   66, 127
    preferences   42
    Web documents   33
        without displaying   34
Scanning   97
Screen
    background   57, 62
    customizing   56
    uncluttering   27–28
Scripps Institution of Oceanography   73
Sea World/Busch Gardens   73
Search engines
    accessing   43, 46
    brokers   113
    CUI W3 Catalog   115–16
    Glimpse indexer   113
    Harvest   113
    Lycos   114
    WebCrawler   112
    World Wide Web Worm   115
Searching
    Boolean   110
    directories   85–87
    guidelines   111
    Internet users   43, 87–88
    keyword   110
    phrases   111
    relevance score   113
    string   31, 110
    types   110–11
        results compared   116
    wildcard characters   115
    words in current document   31

Security   49–50, 59–60
    explanation   44
    proxies   60
    specific page information   35
    viewing secure page   127
Service providers   12
Setup   20–21
    pages   35–36
    printer   31, 36
    See also Preferences
Shakespeare online   82–83
Shell account   16–18
Shopping on Web   120
Show Directory buttons   41
Show FTP file information   41
Show Location option   41
Show Toolbar option   41
SILS Clearinghouse   74
Sliding Tiles Puzzles   122
SLIP (Serial Line Internet Protocol)   12
Smithsonian   72
Software requirements   12–14
Sound
    See Audio files
Sound Machine   68
Source code
    displaying/editing   59
    printing   31
    viewing   38, 91–92
    See also HTML
Source option   38
Sparkle   67
Special Internet Connections   89
Sports Web sites   71
Starting Netscape   22–23
Status indicator (logo)   50
Stock Market Updates   76
Stop
    menu option   39
    toolbar button   31
Stopping document load   31, 39

String searching   31, 110
StuffIt Expander   13
    installing   19
Styles preferences   56–57
Support services for Netscape   45

T

Tags (HTML)   92–96
TCP error encountered...(error message)   131
TCP/IP   12–13
TELNET   59, 82–83
    preferences   21
Threaded news articles   84
.TIFF files   64
    See also Images
Time-Life Publishing   70
Title bar   48
Too many users (error message)   130
Toolbar   28–31
    Back button   23, 29
    clearing from screen   28
    customizing   56
    displaying   41
    Find button   31
    Forward button   29
    Home button   29
    Images button   30
    Open button   30
    Print button   31
    Reload button   29–30
    Stop button   31
Travel Web sites   77–78
    Arctic Adventours, Inc.   120
    Paris   121
    Travels with Samantha   118
    Virtual Tourist   120
Travels with Samantha   118
Trying to locate host...(message)   22

U

Unable to locate server (error message)   129
Undocumented features   125–27
Uniform Resource Locators
    See URL addresses
University of Michigan   74
Unpacking Netscape   19
Updates to Netscape   88–89
URL addresses   23
    "about"   126
    accessible with Netscape   79
    defined   10
    displayed for active links   49
    displaying current   20, 41
    entering   30, 47–48
    failing   48
    going directly to   30, 32, 39
    http   79
    random selection   123
    viewing complete   48
URouLette   123
U.S. Census Information Server   76
U.S. Constitution   119
U.S. Government Master Page   74–75
USENET news groups
    See Newsgroups

V

VIBE   70
Video files
    preferences   21
    viewing   66–67
    Web sites   77
    See also Helper applications
View All Newsgroups button   84–85
    absent   127
View Bookmarks option   40
View History option   39
View menu   37–38

Village Schoolhouse   73
Virtual Frogs   73–74
Virtual Hospital   118
Virtual Radio   122
Virtual Tourist   120

W

Washington Weekly   70
Weather Maps/Movies   121
Web
    See World Wide Web
Web browsers
    See Browsers of Web
Web pages
    See Home pages; Pages
Web searchers
    See Search engines
WebCrawler   112
WebLint   104
WebLouvre
    See WebMuseum, Paris
WebMuseum, Paris   24, 72
    downloading from   103–4
What's Cool?
    directory button   46
    menu option   42
What's New?
    directory button   45
    menu option   42
White House   75
Whole Internet User's Guide   44
Wildcard searching   115
Windows
    closing   36
    enlarging   65
    multiple   32, 59
World Wide Web
    best page design   117–23
    creating pages
        See HTML

defined 9
future 124
growth 2
history 1–2
how it works 4–5
information about 89
searching
   See Search engines; Searching
staying current 88–90
World Wide Web Virtual Library Home Page
   Directory 78–79
World Wide Web Worm 115
WWW
   See World Wide Web

 Y

Yanoff, Scott 89

 Z

Zines 70

COLOPHON

This book was developed on a Power Macintosh 8100/80. All pages were produced in Aldus PageMaker 5.0. Some graphics were produced or edited in Adobe Photoshop 3.0 and Adobe Illustrator 5.0. Chapter titles are set in Anna. Chapter numbers are set in Futura Condensed Bold. The body text is Palatino with Futura Heavy subheads. Tables and sidebars are set in Futura. The title of the book (on the cover and title pages) is set in Michelangelo.

Internet Resources

The Mac Internet Tour Guide, Second Edition
$29.95, 432 pages, illustrated

This runaway bestseller has been updated to include Enhanced Mosaic, the hot new Web reader, along with graphical software for e-mail, file downloading, newsreading and more. Noted for its down-to-earth documentation, the new edition features expanded listings and a look at new Net developments.

America Online's Internet, Windows Edition
$24.95, 328 pages, illustrated

AOL members can now slide onto the Infobahn with a mere mouse-click. This quick-start for AOL Interent newcomers explains e-mail, downloading files, reading newsgroups and joining mailing lists. The companion disk includes AOL software and 10 hours of free online time (for new members only).

Internet Virtual Worlds Quick Tour
$14.00, 224 pages, illustrated

Learn to locate and master real-time interactive communication forums and games by participating in the virtual worlds of MUD (Multi-User Dimension) and MOO (MUD Object-Oriented). *Internet Virtual Worlds Quick Tour* introduces users to the basic functions by defining different categories (individual, interactive and both) and detailing standard protocols. Also revealed is the insider's lexicon of these mysterious cyberworlds.

Internet Roadside Attractions

$29.95, 384 pages, illustrated

Why take the word of one when you can get a quorum? Seven experienced Internauts share their favorite Web sites, Gophers, FTP sites, chats, games, newsgroups and mailing lists. For easy browsing, attractions are listed by category, with in-depth descriptions. The companion CD-ROM contains the entire text of the book, hyperlinked for off-line browsing and online Web-hopping.

Internet E-Mail Quick Tour

$14.00, 152 pages, illustrated

Whether it's the Internet or an online service, most people use their connections primarily for electronic messaging. This all-in-one guide to getting it right includes tips on software, security, style and Netiquette. Also included: how to obtain an e-mail account, useful addresses, interesting mailing lists and more!

Internet Chat Quick Tour

$14.00, 200 pages, illustrated

Global conversations in real-time are an integral part of the Internet. The worldwide chat network is where users find online help and forums on the latest scientific research. The *Internet Chat Quick Tour* describes the best software sites for users to chat on a variety of subjects.

Books marked with this logo include a free Internet *Online Companion*™, featuring archives of free utilities plus a software archive and links to other Internet resources.

Insightful Guides

America Online's Internet, Macintosh Edition
$24.95, 336 pages, illustrated

Access the Internet with the simple click of a mouse. This quick-start for AOL newcomers explains how to use e-mail, download files, read newsgroups and join mailing lists. A companion disk includes ready-to-install AOL software and 10 hours of free online time (for new members only).

The Mac Shareware 500, Second Edition
$34.95, 496 pages, illustrated

This book is a fantastic reference for any designer or desktop publisher interested in saving money by using the vast resources shareware offers. Literally thousands of fonts, graphics, clip-art files and utilities are available for downloading via dozens of online services. To get you started, this book includes two disks of shareware.

Mac, Word & Excel Desktop Companion, Second Edition
$24.95, 362 pages, illustrated

Why clutter your desktop with three guides? This money saver gets you up and running with Apple's System 7.1 software and the latest versions of Microsoft Word and Excel for the Mac. A complete overview, examples of each program's commands, tools and features, and step-by-step tutorials guide you easily along the learning curve to maximum Macintosh productivity.

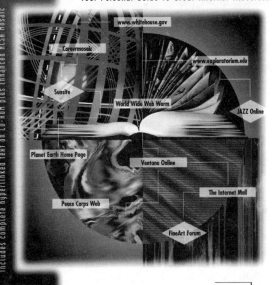

To order any Ventana Press title, complete this order form and mail or fax it to us, with payment, for quick shipment.

TITLE	ISBN	Quantity		Price		Total
America Online's Internet, Macintosh Edition	1-56604-175-9	_____	x	$24.95	=	$ _____
Internet Chat Quick Tour	1-56604-223-2	_____	x	$14.00	=	$ _____
Internet E-Mail Quick Tour	1-56604-220-8	_____	x	$14.00	=	$ _____
Internet Roadside Attractions	1-56604-193-7	_____	x	$29.95	=	$ _____
Internet Virtual Worlds Quick Tour	1-56604-222-4	_____	x	$14.00	=	$ _____
Looking Good in Print, 3rd Edition	1-56604-047-7	_____	x	$24.95	=	$ _____
The Mac Internet Tour Guide, 2nd Edition	1-56604-173-2	_____	x	$29.95	=	$ _____
The Mac Shareware 500, 2nd Edition	1-56604-076-0	_____	x	$34.95	=	$ _____
Mac, Word & Excel Desktop Companion, 2nd Edition	1-56604-130-9	_____	x	$24.95	=	$ _____
Netscape Quick Tour for Macintosh	1-56604-248-8	_____	x	$14.00	=	$ _____
The System 7.5 Book, 3rd Edition	1-56604-129-5	_____	x	$24.95	=	$ _____
Voodoo Mac, 2nd Edition	1-56604-177-5	_____	x	$24.95	=	$ _____
Walking the World Wide Web	1-56604-208-9	_____	x	$29.95	=	$ _____

Subtotal = $ _____
Shipping = $ _____
TOTAL = $ _____

SHIPPING:

For all standard orders, please ADD $4.50/first book, $1.35/each additional.
For "two-day air," ADD $8.25/first book, $2.25/each additional.
For orders to Canada, ADD $6.50/book.
For orders sent C.O.D., ADD $4.50 to your shipping rate.
North Carolina residents must ADD 6% sales tax.
International orders require additional shipping charges.

Name _____ Daytime telephone _____

Company _____

Address (No PO Box) _____

City _____ State _____ Zip _____

____ Payment enclosed ____VISA ____ MC Acc't # _____ Exp. date _____

Exact name on card _____ Signature _____

Mail to: Ventana Press, PO Box 2468, Chapel Hill, NC 27515 ☎ 800/743-5369 Fax 919/942-1140